Slimming World's
one for all

one-pot *wonders...*

If you love nothing more than tucking into delicious Food Optimising meals – and like nothing less than washing up lots of pots afterwards – this is the book for you!

Every one of these mouth-watering all-in-one meals will take you one step closer to your weight-loss dream using just one piece of cookware (although if you feel like adding mash, rice or extra Speed veg, go right ahead!).

Oven-roasted recipes like chicken enchilada bake will make your roasting tin or baking tray shine, while saucy sensations like tomato soup with turkey meatballs are perfect for your saucepan or casserole. Break out the frying pan or wok for treats like seafood sizzle with salsa verde – and if you've discovered the joy of slow cookers, dishes like Asian barbecue chicken are definitely worth the wait!

you'll want to try them all
— one by one!

from a
flash in the pan
to **slow and steady,**
we've catered for
everything!

tray-mendous!

You'll be the host with the roast when you serve up temptations such as jumbo koftas and cheesy colcannon potato skins, all cooked using just a baking tray, roasting tin or ovenproof dish.

jumbo koftas
with mediterranean veg

serves 4
Free
ready in 50 minutes

Half meatball, half burger, these bumper-sized koftas will delight everyone, and we've served them on a bed of veg brimming with Mediterranean sunshine.

50g dried bulgar wheat

750g lean beef mince (5% fat or less)

1 tsp dried chilli flakes

1½ tbsp cumin seeds

½ tsp ground cinnamon

½ tbsp dried mint

4 garlic cloves, crushed

small pack fresh parsley, finely chopped

4 peppers (any colours), deseeded and cut into small chunks

2 large courgettes, sliced

2 medium red onions, cut into wedges

1 large aubergine, cut into small chunks

3 large tomatoes, cut into wedges

150g fat-free natural Greek yogurt

1 tbsp sumac or lemon juice

Put the bulgar wheat in a small heatproof bowl, cover generously with boiling water and leave to soak for 10 minutes. Drain well, tip on to a clean tea towel and squeeze out the excess water.

Preheat the oven to 230°C/fan 210°C/gas 8.

Put the beef in a mixing bowl and add the bulgar wheat, chilli flakes, cumin seeds, cinnamon, dried mint, two-thirds of the garlic, almost all of the parsley, ¾ tsp salt and plenty of black pepper. Mix well with your hands then divide the mixture into 12 portions and form each portion into a rugby ball shape.

Put the peppers, courgettes, onions, aubergine and some salt and pepper in a large, non-stick deep-sided baking tray or roasting tin (about 36cm x 26cm). Add 3 tbsp water and toss well then spread out in an even layer and roast for 10 minutes.

Remove the tray from the oven, add a splash more water if needed and toss well. Scatter over the tomato wedges and rest the beef koftas on top. Return to the oven for 15-20 minutes or until the koftas are cooked through and the vegetables are tender.

Meanwhile, stir the remaining garlic into the yogurt and divide between 4 small bowls.

Sprinkle the remaining parsley and the sumac or lemon juice over the koftas, vegetables and garlic yogurt to serve.

roasted sausage supper

serves 4

Free

ready in 1 hour

low-calorie cooking spray

2 medium onions, cut into wedges

3 large red peppers, deseeded and cut into small chunks

2 small fennel bulbs, trimmed and cut into wedges

4 garlic cloves, sliced

500g new potatoes, scrubbed and halved lengthways

1 tbsp chopped fresh rosemary, plus sprigs to garnish

12 Slimming World Syn-free Pork Sausages (or see tip)

mustard powder made up with water, to serve

The sausages are the stars in this easy Free bake, while fennel and rosemary bring a fabulous aroma.

Preheat your oven to 220°C/fan 200°C/gas 7.

Spray a very large, non-stick deep-sided baking tray or roasting tin (about 40cm x 30cm) with low-calorie cooking spray (if you don't have non-stick, line your tray or tin with non-stick baking paper). Add the onions, peppers, fennel, garlic, potatoes, rosemary, ½ tsp salt and some pepper and toss well. Spread out in an even layer and roast for 20 minutes.

Remove the tray from the oven, turn the vegetables and add the sausages. Roast for a further 25-30 minutes or until the sausages are cooked through and lightly browned, turning them halfway. Check that the vegetables are tender and give them a bit longer in the oven if necessary.

Garnish with rosemary sprigs and serve with the mustard.

If you can't get Slimming World sausages, use other low-fat sausages and count the Syns.

smoky pork steaks with winter veg

serves 4

Free

ready in 1 hour

We've put Spanish-spiced pork together with a delicious medley of winter root vegetables – perfect for warming your cockles!

2 garlic cloves, crushed

½ tbsp smoked paprika

1 tsp roughly chopped fresh thyme

1 tsp chopped fresh rosemary

2 tbsp cider vinegar or white wine vinegar

8 small pork loin steaks, visible fat removed

low-calorie cooking spray

450g celeriac, peeled and cut into small chunks

2 large parsnips, peeled and cut into small chunks

1 large sweet potato, peeled and cut into small chunks

1 tsp caraway seeds

½ Savoy cabbage, cored, leaves sliced

2 large leeks, thickly sliced

6 smoked back bacon rashers, visible fat removed, roughly chopped

Mix the garlic, paprika, thyme, rosemary, vinegar and some seasoning in a small bowl. Rub the mixture over both sides of each pork steak and set aside. (For the best flavour, do this a few hours ahead – ideally overnight – and chill in the fridge.)

Preheat your oven to 220°C/fan 200°C/gas 7.

Spray a very large, non-stick deep-sided baking tray or roasting tin (about 40cm x 30cm) with low-calorie cooking spray and add the celeriac, parsnips, sweet potato, caraway seeds, ½ tsp salt and some pepper and toss well. Spread out in an even layer and roast for 20 minutes.

Meanwhile, put the cabbage in a heatproof bowl, cover with boiling water and leave for 5 minutes. Drain and dry well on a clean tea towel.

Remove the tray from the oven and stir in the cabbage, leeks and bacon. Spray with a little more low-calorie cooking spray and lay the pork steaks on top. Roast for a further 20-25 minutes or until the pork steaks are cooked through and the vegetables are tender. Serve hot.

For a hint of sweetness, add 2 level tsp maple syrup to the pork marinade (adds ½ Syn per serving)

herby lamb
with baked ratatouille

serves 4

Free

ready in 50 minutes

---

4 lean lamb leg steaks,
visible fat removed

6 garlic cloves, finely chopped

2 tsp dried oregano

1 large red onion,
roughly chopped

1 large aubergine, cut into
small chunks

2 large courgettes,
roughly chopped

2 large red peppers, deseeded
and cut into small chunks

1 small fennel bulb, trimmed and
thickly sliced

4 plum tomatoes, quartered
lengthways

1 tbsp red wine vinegar

fresh basil leaves, to serve

Ratatouille is a classic French veg recipe and it goes brilliantly with these luscious lamb steaks.

Sprinkle both sides of the lamb steaks with a little of the garlic, half the oregano and some seasoning and set aside on a plate. (For the best flavour, do this a few hours ahead – ideally overnight – and chill in the fridge.)

Preheat your oven to 220°C/fan 200°C/gas 7.

Put all the vegetables, remaining garlic and oregano, ½ tsp salt and some pepper in a very large, non-stick deep-sided baking tray or roasting tin (about 40cm x 30 cm). Add 3 tbsp water, toss well and spread out in an even layer. Roast for 25-30 minutes or until almost tender, turning halfway and adding a splash of water if needed.

Remove the tray from the oven and add a splash more water. Turn the vegetables and lay the lamb steaks on top. Return the tray to the oven and roast for a further 10-15 minutes or until the lamb is just cooked and the vegetables are tender.

Sprinkle the vinegar over the vegetables, check the seasoning and scatter over the basil to serve.

chicken enchilada bake

Your friends and family will go loco for this Food Optimising-friendly makeover of the much-loved Mexican meal!

Preheat your oven to 200°C/fan 180°C/gas 6.

Put the peppers, onions, ½ tsp chilli flakes, ½ tsp salt and some pepper in a large, non-stick baking tray, roasting tin or ovenproof dish (about 36cm x 26cm). Add 3 tbsp water, toss well and spread out in an even layer. Roast for 25 minutes, turning everything halfway and adding a splash more water if needed.

Remove the tray from the oven and stir in the sweetcorn and black beans. Lightly season the chicken breasts and arrange on top of the vegetables. Mix the passata with the tomato purée, garlic, cumin, sweetener and the remaining chilli flakes. Pour the mixture over everything, cover with foil and roast for another 30 minutes.

Uncover, return to the oven and bake for 10 minutes or until the sauce has reduced and thickened and the chicken has cooked through.

Remove the tray from the oven, sprinkle over the cheese and spring onions and return to the oven for 5 minutes or until the cheese has just melted. Serve hot with the lettuce and quark.

serves 4

3 Syns per serving

ready in 1½ hours

---

3 large peppers (any colours), deseeded and cut into small chunks

2 large red onions, roughly chopped

½ tbsp dried chilli flakes

325g can sweetcorn kernels in water, drained

400g can or carton black beans, drained and rinsed

4 skinless and boneless chicken breasts

500g passata

2 tbsp tomato purée

1 large garlic clove, crushed

2 tsp ground cumin

½ level tsp sweetener granules

80g reduced-fat Cheddar cheese, coarsely grated

4 spring onions, thinly sliced

shredded lettuce, to serve

plain quark, to serve

serves 4

Free

ready in 1½ hours,
plus marinating

1½ tbsp lime juice, plus slices or wedges to serve

1 tbsp paprika, plus extra for the raita

4 chicken legs, skinned

7.5cm piece fresh root ginger, peeled and thinly sliced

seeds of 8 green cardamom pods, crushed

2 tbsp garam masala

1 tsp turmeric

6 garlic cloves, crushed

250g fat-free natural Greek yogurt, plus 150g for the raita

3 large floury potatoes, peeled and cut into small chunks

3 medium parsnips, peeled and cut into small chunks

1 large cauliflower, cut into small florets

100g frozen peas, thawed in warm water and drained

low-calorie cooking spray

1 tbsp curry powder (mild or medium)

2 tsp cumin seeds

¼ small cucumber, grated

½ small pack fresh mint, chopped

4 large tomatoes, roughly chopped

tandoori chicken with bombay veg

The irresistible aroma of curry in your kitchen will let everyone know that something special is coming soon… a fab fakeaway that's completely Free!

Put the lime juice, paprika and ½ tsp salt in a wide bowl and mix well. Slash both sides of each chicken leg with a sharp knife and add to the bowl, turning to coat well. Cover and set aside for 30 minutes.

Put the ginger, cardamom seeds, garam masala, turmeric, almost all of the garlic and 4 tbsp yogurt into a small food processor and blend to a paste. Stir the mixture into the remaining yogurt, mix well and pour all over the chicken legs to coat them completely. Cover and chill for at least 1 hour (or ideally up to 6 hours if you have time).

Preheat the oven to 230°C/fan 210°C/gas 8.

Put the potatoes, parsnips, cauliflower and peas in a very large, non-stick deep-sided baking tray or roasting tin (about 40cm x 30cm), spray with low-calorie cooking spray and toss well. Mix the curry powder and cumin seeds with ½ tsp salt, sprinkle over the vegetables and toss again to coat well. Spread out the veg in an even layer and roast for 25 minutes.

Remove the vegetables from the oven and turn them over. Lift the chicken legs from their marinade, shaking off any excess, and add them to the tray. Return to the oven and roast for another 35-40 minutes or until the chicken is cooked and the vegetables are tender, turning the chicken halfway.

Meanwhile, make the raita. Mix the extra yogurt and remaining garlic with the cucumber, most of the mint and some salt. Sprinkle with paprika.

Divide the veg between plates and scatter over the tomatoes and remaining mint. Top with the chicken legs and serve hot with lime slices or wedges and the raita.

gremolata chicken

This spectacular Free chicken dinner couldn't be simpler to make, and the Italian gremolata topping adds a delicious touch of luxury.

Preheat the oven to 220°C/fan 200°C/gas 7.

Arrange the leeks, carrots and courgettes in a very large, non-stick deep-sided baking tray or roasting tin (about 40cm x 30cm). Cut the top off the garlic bulb (like you would with a Hallowe'en pumpkin lid) to reveal the cloves and add the bulb to the tray. Sprinkle over the thyme leaves and add 3 tbsp water and half the lemon juice. Season lightly, mix well and roast for 25 minutes, turning halfway and adding another splash of water if needed.

Meanwhile, skin each drumstick by pulling away a bit of skin at the thick end (use kitchen paper to get a good grip) and pulling it off over the bony end. Put the drumsticks in a bowl and sprinkle with the cayenne pepper, remaining lemon juice and a little salt.

Give the vegetables a stir and add a splash more water. Nestle the chicken drumsticks among them and roast for a further 35 minutes or until the vegetables are golden and the chicken is cooked through, adding more water if needed. Leave to rest for 5 minutes.

Make the gremolata by combining the parsley and lemon zest in a small bowl. Scatter the gremolata over the chicken and veg and serve hot. Delicious with mashed potatoes – or swede mash if you want to keep it suitable for Extra Easy *SP*.

Serve the garlic bulb as a garnish or squeeze the flesh from the cloves, mash well and stir through the vegetables.

serves 4

Free

ready in 1 hour 15 minutes

3 leeks, sliced

3 carrots, peeled and sliced

3 courgettes, sliced

1 garlic bulb

2 tsp fresh thyme leaves

grated zest of 1 unwaxed lemon, plus 2 tbsp juice

12 chicken drumsticks

1 tsp cayenne pepper

4 tbsp chopped fresh parsley

one-tray sunday roast

serves 4

1 Syn per serving

ready in 1 hour 10 minutes

---

low-calorie cooking spray

8 skinless chicken thighs

500g Charlotte potatoes, scrubbed and halved lengthways

500g Chantenay carrots, scrubbed

½ swede, peeled and cut into small chunks

2 medium onions, cut into wedges

250g Brussels sprouts, trimmed

1 tbsp roughly chopped fresh thyme leaves, plus extra to serve

6 Slimming World Syn-free Pork Sausages (or see tip)

4 back bacon rashers, visible fat removed, halved or roughly chopped

25g dried chicken gravy granules

1 tsp chicken liquid stock concentrate

For Sunday lunch without the fuss, this one-tray, one-Syn wonder is the recipe you've always wanted. It would also make a fabulously easy Christmas dinner!

Preheat your oven to 220°C/fan 200°C/gas 7.

Spray a very large, non-stick deep-sided baking tray or roasting tin (about 40cm x 30cm) with low-calorie cooking spray. Add the chicken, potatoes, carrots, swede, onions, sprouts, thyme, ½ tsp salt and some black pepper and toss well. Spread out in an even layer and roast for 45 minutes, adding the sausages for the last 20 minutes.

Remove the tray from the oven and turn the vegetables. Lay the bacon on top of the chicken, return to the oven and roast for a further 10 minutes or until the chicken, sausages and bacon are cooked and the vegetables are tender.

Shortly before your roast is ready, put the gravy granules in a heatproof jug with the chicken liquid stock concentrate. Add 280ml boiling water and whisk well.

Halve the sausages, divide everything between plates, scatter over the extra thyme and serve hot with the gravy.

If you can't get Slimming World sausages, use other low-fat sausages and count the Syns.

burmese baked chicken thighs

serves 4

2 Syns per serving

ready in 1½ hours

---

seeds of 8 green cardamom pods

5 shallots (or 2 echalion shallots), sliced

6 garlic cloves, peeled

3cm piece fresh root ginger, peeled and sliced

2 lemongrass stalks, outer leaves discarded, sliced

2 medium-hot red chillies, deseeded

2 tsp turmeric

1 tbsp paprika

2 tsp curry powder (heat to your taste)

200ml reduced-fat coconut milk

zest and juice of 1 unwaxed lemon

400g can chopped tomatoes

1 butternut squash, peeled, deseeded and cut into small chunks

225g can bamboo shoots, drained

8 large skinless chicken thighs

chopped fresh coriander, to serve

Creamy coconut milk and a host of warming spices give this simple curry a beautifully complex flavour.

Preheat the oven to 180°C/fan 160°C/gas 4.

Put the cardamom seeds in a small food processor with the shallots, garlic, ginger, lemongrass, chillies, turmeric, paprika, curry powder, 2 tbsp coconut milk and ½ tsp salt and blend to a smooth paste.

Mix your spice paste with the lemon zest and juice, chopped tomatoes and remaining coconut milk in a bowl.

Scatter the squash and bamboo shoots in a large non-stick baking tray or roasting tin (about 36cm x 26cm). Season lightly, toss well and spread out in an even layer. Place the chicken thighs on top and pour over the coconut sauce. Bake for 1 hour 15 minutes, turning the thighs after 40 minutes.

Scatter over the coriander and serve hot.

cajun fish
with pineapple salsa

serves 4

Free

ready in 25 minutes

---

1 tbsp Cajun seasoning

1 tsp dried parsley

1 tsp dried oregano

4 large boneless firm white fish fillets (such as sea bass, tilapia or sea bream)

2 tbsp lime juice

low-calorie cooking spray

2 baby cos lettuces or 1 romaine lettuce heart, shredded

for the pineapple salsa

75g prepared fresh pineapple, diced

75g baby sweetcorn, thinly sliced

75g cucumber, halved lengthways, deseeded and diced

1 small red onion, finely chopped

1 medium-hot red chilli, deseeded and chopped

100g radishes, sliced

½ small pack fresh coriander, chopped

Enjoy the summer all year round with this speedy combo of oven-baked fish and a fresh, punchy salsa.

Preheat your oven to 200°C/fan 180°C/gas 6 and rest a rack in a large baking tray or roasting tin (about 36cm x 26cm).

Mix the Cajun seasoning, parsley, oregano, ½ tsp salt and some black pepper in a small bowl.

Sprinkle the fish fillets on both sides with half of the lime juice followed by the spice and herb mix. Spray with low-calorie cooking spray and arrange on the rack, skin-side down. Bake for 12-15 minutes or until just cooked through.

Meanwhile, put all the salsa ingredients except the coriander in a bowl, add the remaining lime juice and stir well. Add salt to taste and stir in the coriander just before serving.

Divide the shredded lettuce between plates. Lay the fish fillets on top and spoon over the salsa to serve.

Swap the pineapple for diced melon, watermelon or another Speed fruit to make this meal perfect for Extra Easy ⟨SP⟩.

thyme-baked trout with asparagus

serves 4

Free

ready in 40 minutes

Seasonal asparagus goes brilliantly with fresh trout in this delicious recipe – eat outdoors for best results!

low-calorie cooking spray

750g new potatoes, scrubbed and halved lengthways

2 garlic cloves, finely chopped

1 tbsp chopped fresh thyme or lemon thyme leaves

4 large or 8 small boneless rainbow trout fillets

1 tbsp lemon juice, plus 1 small lemon, sliced

700g asparagus spears, woody ends trimmed (you'll need about 600g prepared)

300g cherry tomatoes, halved

Preheat the oven to 220°C/fan 200°C/gas 7.

Spray a very large, non-stick deep-sided baking tray or roasting tin (about 40cm x 30cm) with low-calorie cooking spray and add the potatoes, half the garlic, half the thyme or lemon thyme and some salt and pepper. Toss well and spread out in an even layer. Slide into the oven and roast for 15 minutes.

Meanwhile, rub the trout fillets on both sides with the lemon juice and season lightly. Sprinkle the fleshy side with the remaining garlic and thyme or lemon thyme and top with the lemon slices. Put the asparagus into a shallow dish with the tomatoes, spray with low-calorie cooking spray, season and turn to coat well.

Remove the tray from the oven, turn the potatoes over and push to one side. Put the asparagus spears on the other side and return to the oven for 5-6 minutes, depending on their thickness, until they are almost tender.

Remove the tray from the oven, turn the asparagus and lay the trout fillets on top, skin-side down. Scatter the tomatoes around the fish and roast for 8-10 minutes or until the vegetables are tender and the trout is just cooked through. Serve hot.

spicy salmon
and squash bake

serves 4

2 Syns per serving

ready in 1 hour 15 minutes

The colours and fragrance of this easy fish dish will pull you in and the flavours will bring you back for more!

200ml boiling vegetable or chicken stock

200ml reduced-fat coconut milk

4 fresh or dried kaffir lime leaves, halved

2 lemongrass stalks, outer leaves discarded, finely chopped

3cm piece fresh root ginger, peeled and finely chopped

2 garlic cloves, finely chopped

1 medium-hot red chilli, deseeded and finely chopped

1 large butternut squash, peeled, deseeded and thinly sliced

4 large skinless and boneless salmon fillets

1 tbsp lime juice

chopped fresh coriander, to serve

light soy sauce, to serve (optional)

Preheat the oven to 190°C/fan 170°C/gas 5.

Put the stock, coconut milk and kaffir lime leaves into a microwave-proof jug and heat on high for 1-2 minutes or until boiling.

Meanwhile, mix the lemongrass, ginger, garlic, chilli and a little salt and pepper in a small bowl.

Layer half of the squash in a medium non-stick baking tray, roasting tin or ovenproof dish (about 33cm x 23cm) and sprinkle with one-third of the lemongrass mixture. Pour over half of the stock mixture and repeat the layers, finishing with the rest of the stock. Cover with foil and bake for 30 minutes. Remove the foil and return the tray to the oven for another 15 minutes.

Meanwhile, put the salmon on a plate and sprinkle over the lime juice and some seasoning.

Remove the tray from the oven and place the salmon fillets on top, skinned-side down. Sprinkle with the remaining lemongrass mixture and bake for a further 12-15 minutes or until the salmon is just cooked through and the squash is tender.

Scatter with coriander, sprinkle with a little light soy sauce, if using, and serve hot.

roasted cauliflower cheese

serves 4

3 Syns per serving

ready in 1 hour

There's no better way to enjoy a cauliflower. We've added cherry tomatoes to the old favourite for an extra burst of freshness and flavour.

2 large cauliflowers, broken into large florets

low-calorie cooking spray

300g cherry tomatoes

250g plain quark

1 medium egg, beaten

1 level tsp Dijon mustard

75g reduced-fat Cheddar cheese, grated

chopped fresh chives, to serve

Preheat the oven to 200°C/fan 180°C/gas 6.

Put the cauliflower florets in a large, non-stick baking tray, roasting tin or ovenproof dish (about 36cm x 26cm). Spray with low-calorie cooking spray, season lightly and toss well. Roast for 35-40 minutes or until almost tender and nicely tinged with brown.

Remove the tray from the oven, turn the florets and scatter over the cherry tomatoes. Return to the oven and roast for a further 10 minutes or until the tomatoes and cauliflower are tender.

Preheat the grill to high.

Mix the quark with the egg, mustard, half of the cheese and a little seasoning. Pour the mixture evenly over the cauliflower and tomatoes and spread out to cover. Scatter over the rest of the cheese and grill for 2-3 minutes or until the sauce has heated through and the cheese is melted and golden. Scatter over the chives and serve with salad if you like.

one for all | **tray-mendous!**

okra and chickpea curry

serves 4

Free

Ⓥ **vegan** (without the yogurt)

ready in 1 hour 10 minutes

---

1 large potato, peeled and cut into small chunks

1 large aubergine, cut into small chunks

1 small cauliflower, cut into small florets

350g okra, halved

2 medium onions, chopped

1 tbsp cumin seeds

6 garlic cloves, 4 finely chopped and 2 crushed

3cm piece of fresh root ginger, peeled and grated

2 chillies (red or green), deseeded and finely chopped

3 tbsp mild or medium curry powder, plus a pinch to serve

400g can chickpeas

2 tbsp tomato purée

2 x 400g cans chopped tomatoes

150g fat-free natural Greek yogurt

juice of 1 small lemon

From filling chickpeas to soothing spices, there's so much going on in this unforgettable oven-cooked curry.

Preheat your oven to 220°C/fan 200°C/gas 7.

Put the potato, aubergine, cauliflower, okra, onions, cumin seeds, ½ tsp salt and some pepper in a very large, non-stick deep-sided baking tray or roasting tin (about 40cm x 30cm). Add a few tbsp water, toss well, spread out in an even layer and roast for 20 minutes, tossing again and adding a splash more water halfway.

Remove the tray from the oven and add the chopped garlic, ginger, chillies and curry powder. Gently stir everything together and return to the oven for 5 minutes.

Meanwhile, drain the liquid from the chickpea can into a bowl and whisk in the tomato purée.

Remove the tray from the oven and add the chopped tomatoes, tomato purée mixture and chickpeas and stir well. Shake the tray to level the ingredients and return to the oven for 30 minutes or until the sauce has reduced and the vegetables are tender.

Meanwhile, stir the crushed garlic into the yogurt, add the lemon juice and salt to taste, and sprinkle with a pinch of curry powder.

Remove the tray from the oven and serve with the garlic yogurt.

provençal vegetables with pesto

serves 4

Free (for the vegetables)

1 Syn per level tbsp (for the pesto)

Ⓥ (if the cheese is vegetarian) *SP*

ready in 50 minutes

---

3 medium red onions, cut into wedges

500g beetroot, peeled and cut into wedges (or use vacuum-packed beetroot and add with the lentils)

3 large courgettes, thickly sliced

400g can artichoke hearts, drained and halved

150g cherry tomatoes

400g can green lentils, drained and rinsed

for the pesto

40g fresh basil leaves

15g pine nuts

1 large garlic clove, crushed

finely grated zest and juice of ½ small unwaxed lemon

4 level tbsp freshly grated Parmesan cheese or vegetarian alternative

Give your roasted vegetables the red carpet treatment with an indulgent drizzle of pesto.

Preheat your oven to 220°C/fan 200°C/gas 7.

Put the onions, beetroot, courgettes, ½ tsp salt and some pepper in a very large, non-stick deep-sided baking tray or roasting tin (about 40cm x 30cm). Add 3 tbsp water, toss well and spread out in an even layer. Slide into the oven and roast for 30 minutes, turning the vegetables occasionally and adding a splash more water if needed.

Meanwhile, make the pesto. Put the basil, pine nuts, garlic, lemon zest and juice plus 8 tbsp water into a food processor and blend to a paste. Stir in the cheese and salt to taste.

Remove the tray from the oven, add the artichoke hearts, cherry tomatoes and lentils and turn the vegetables over to mix. Spread out once more, return to the oven and roast for a further 8-10 minutes or until the vegetables are tender and the artichokes and lentils have heated through.

Drizzle with the pesto to serve.

If you don't use all the pesto, save some and stir it into cooked dried pasta for a speedy meal. It'll keep in the fridge for 3 days and can be frozen in ice cube trays, wrapped in a sealable bag.

one for all | **tray-mendous!**

cheesy colcannon potato skins

serves 4

3 Syns per serving

ready in 1 hour 40 minutes

4 large baking potatoes

low-calorie cooking spray

2 medium onions, halved and thinly sliced

150g spring cabbage or spring greens, shredded

150g plain quark

80g reduced-fat Cheddar cheese, coarsely grated

3 small tomatoes, chopped

We've made good old jacket potatoes even better by stuffing them with Irish colcannon and magnificently melty Cheddar cheese.

Preheat the oven to 220°C/fan 200°C/gas 7.

Prick each potato 2-3 times with the tip of a sharp knife, pop them straight on to an oven shelf and bake for 1 hour 15 minutes or until tender with a crisp skin.

Meanwhile, spray a medium non-stick baking tray or roasting tin (about 33cm x 23cm) with low-calorie cooking spray, add the onions and some seasoning and toss well. Spread out in an even layer and roast alongside the potatoes for 15-20 minutes or until soft and nicely caramelised. Remove and set aside.

Put the cabbage or spring greens in a heatproof bowl and cover with boiling water. Stand for 5 minutes then drain and dry well on a clean tea towel.

Remove the potatoes from the oven and halve them lengthways. Scoop the potato flesh into the heatproof bowl, mash roughly and stir in the quark, roasted onions, cabbage or spring greens, half the cheese and some seasoning to taste. Wipe the baking tray.

Spoon the mixture back into the potato skins and lay them on the baking tray. Scatter over the tomatoes, sprinkle with the remaining cheese and bake for 15 minutes or until the cheese is golden. Serve hot with salad.

tuscan kale salad

serves 4

Free

 vegan (if the balsamic vinegar is vegetarian/vegan)

ready in 40 minutes

---

low-calorie cooking spray

600g small salad potatoes, sliced

400g small carrots, peeled and sliced

3 small red onions, cut into wedges

1 tbsp roughly chopped fresh thyme leaves

4 garlic cloves, finely chopped

pinch of dried chilli flakes

400g can cannellini or flageolet beans, drained and rinsed

200g curly kale, torn into bite-size pieces

balsamic vinegar, to serve

Go vegitalian with this simple bake of beans, veggies and more-ish hints of chilli and garlic.

Preheat your oven to 220°C/fan 200°C/gas 7.

Spray a large, non-stick deep-sided baking tray or roasting tin with low-calorie cooking spray and add the potatoes, carrots, onions, thyme, garlic, chilli flakes and some salt and pepper. Toss well and spread out in an even layer. Slide into the oven and roast for 20 minutes.

Remove the tray from the oven, stir in the beans and scatter over the kale. Spray with low-calorie cooking spray and roast for 10 minutes or until the kale is crisp in places.

Divide between plates and drizzle with balsamic vinegar to serve.

Swap the balsamic vinegar for pesto if you like (see page 36 – adds 1 Syn per level tbsp). Bear in mind the pesto isn't suitable for vegans.

pot luck

Nothing says comfort food like a hot pan bubbling away!
Choose from sensations simmered in saucepans and casseroles
like spring pork casserole and captain's chicken curry.

paprika pork

serves 4

Free

ready in 2½ hours

---

low-calorie cooking spray

750g pork fillet (tenderloin), visible fat removed, cut into chunks

2 red onions, halved and thinly sliced

2 garlic cloves, thinly sliced

1 medium-hot red chilli, deseeded and finely chopped

2 tbsp red wine vinegar

1 tsp paprika

4 peppers (any colours), deseeded and sliced

500g baby or new potatoes, scrubbed

50g passata, blended with 250ml boiling water

pinch of saffron (optional)

chopped fresh coriander, to serve

This Spanish-style winter warmer featuring spicy pork and peppers is irresistibly easy!

Preheat your oven to 160°C/fan 140°C/gas 3.

Spray a large non-stick casserole pan with low-calorie cooking spray and place over a medium heat. Season the pork and sear in batches until lightly coloured, transferring each batch to a plate.

Spray the pan with more low-calorie cooking spray, add the onions and fry for 5 minutes or until softened and lightly coloured, stirring often. Add the garlic and chilli and cook for 1 minute, then stir in all the remaining ingredients and return the pork to the pan. Cover and cook in the oven for 1 hour, then stir, cover again and cook for another hour.

Scatter over the coriander and serve hot.

spring pork casserole

serves 4

½ **Syn** per serving

ready in 1 hour 50 minutes

---

low-calorie cooking spray

750g pork fillet (tenderloin),
visible fat removed, cut into
large chunks

6 back bacon rashers, visible fat
removed, cut into thin strips

1 large onion, chopped

1 large green pepper, deseeded
and roughly chopped

2 garlic cloves, crushed

1 level tbsp plain flour

2 tsp mild curry powder

200g can chopped tomatoes

1 tsp dried oregano

200ml boiling chicken stock

2 large leeks, sliced

200g button mushrooms, halved

Our slow-cooked pork pot with a mild curry flavour is ideal for a fresh springtime supper – and just as delicious at other times of the year too!

Preheat the oven to 180°C/fan 160°C/gas 4.

Spray a large non-stick casserole pan with low-calorie cooking spray and place over a high heat. Add half the pork and brown on all sides then transfer to a plate and repeat with the rest of the pork. Fry the bacon briskly for 2 minutes and set aside with the pork.

Add the onion, green pepper and garlic to the pan along with 2 tbsp water. Cover, reduce the heat to low and cook for 10 minutes or until soft.

Uncover and stir in the flour and curry powder, followed by the tomatoes, oregano, stock, ½ tsp salt and some pepper. Bring to the boil over a high heat, stirring, then stir in the pork, bacon and leeks. Cover again and cook in the oven for 1 hour.

Remove the pan from the oven and stir in the mushrooms. Cover again, return to the oven and cook for a further 30 minutes or until the pork is meltingly tender. Serve hot.

middle eastern braised beef

Juicy beef, aromatic herbs and spices, plus loads of tasty Speed vegetables, make this a Food Optimising feast to make again and again.

serves 4

Free

ready in 3½ hours

Preheat the oven to 150°C/fan 130°C/gas 2.

Spray a large non-stick casserole pan with low-calorie cooking spray and place over a high heat. Add half the beef and brown nicely all over, then spoon on to a plate and repeat with the rest of the beef.

Add the onions, garlic and 3 tbsp water to the pan, cover and cook over a low heat for 10 minutes or until soft.

Uncover the pan and stir in the tomato purée, paprika, chilli flakes, rosemary, passata, stock, bay leaves, strips of orange zest, ½ tsp salt and some pepper. Bring to the boil over a high heat, stirring, then stir in the beef, cover and cook in the oven for 2 hours.

Remove the pan from the oven and stir in all the vegetables. Cover again and return to the oven for 1 hour or until everything is tender.

Discard the bay leaves, check the seasoning and scatter with parsley to serve.

low-calorie cooking spray

750g lean casserole/braising steak, visible fat removed, cut into large chunks

2 red onions, cut into wedges

6 large garlic cloves, crushed

4 tbsp tomato purée

1 tsp paprika

1 tsp dried chilli flakes

2 tsp dried rosemary

250g passata

300ml boiling beef stock

4 bay leaves

pared zest of ½ small orange

2 carrots, peeled and sliced

1 fennel bulb, thickly sliced

200g runner beans, each cut into 3-4 pieces

2 courgettes, thickly sliced

2 large tomatoes, halved and thickly sliced

chopped fresh parsley, to serve

beef and broccoli ramen

Our soothing Asian-style soup is full of flavour and goodness – a guilt-free fakeaway to enjoy whenever you feel like it!

Put 2 crushed garlic cloves, the ginger, chilli paste, vinegar, sweetener, oyster sauce, ½ tsp salt and plenty of black pepper in a large bowl and mix it all together. Add the steak, toss to coat well and set aside.

Bring some water to the boil in a large non-stick saucepan or casserole pan over a high heat. Add the noodles and broccoli, cook for 4 minutes then drain and set aside.

Add the beef to the pan and stir-fry for 1-2 minutes or until it has just changed colour. Transfer to a plate.

Pour the stock into the pan, add the soy sauce, remaining garlic and white pak choi stalks and bring to the boil. Stir in the beef, noodles, broccoli and green pak choi leaves and bring back to the boil to heat through, stirring.

Divide between bowls and serve with the spring onions to scatter over.

serves 4

Free

ready in 25 minutes

6 garlic cloves, crushed

3cm piece fresh root ginger, peeled and grated

1 level tsp chilli paste

2 tbsp red wine vinegar

1 level tsp sweetener granules

4 tbsp oyster sauce

500g lean rump steak, visible fat removed, sliced

250g dried medium egg noodles

1 broccoli head, cut into small florets

1 litre boiling beef stock

2 tbsp dark soy sauce

250g pak choi, white and green parts separated, thickly sliced

4 spring onions, halved and shredded

turkish lamb and apricot pilaf

Middle Eastern cookery often uses fruit to give a hint of sweetness – and in this simple rice dish the apricots also bring a lovely splash of colour.

serves 4

1 Syn per serving

ready in 50 minutes

___

low-calorie cooking spray

600g lean lamb leg steaks, visible fat removed, cut into bite-size chunks

1 large onion, chopped

2 small cinnamon sticks, halved

1 large aubergine, cut into small chunks

400ml boiling lamb or chicken stock

250g dried basmati rice

300g apricots, halved, stoned and cut into wedges (or see tip)

100g baby leaf spinach, shredded

½ small pack fresh mint, roughly chopped

Spray a large non-stick casserole pan with low-calorie cooking spray and place over a high heat. Season the lamb and fry until nicely browned all over. Transfer to a plate with a slotted spoon.

Add the onion, cinnamon sticks and 2 tbsp water to the pan, cover and reduce the heat to low. Cook for 10 minutes or until the onion is soft.

Increase the heat to high and stir in the aubergine. Cover again and cook for 2-3 minutes, then uncover once more and stir in the stock, rice, lamb and ½ tsp salt. Bring to the boil then cover, reduce the heat to low and cook for 12 minutes.

Scatter the apricots and spinach on top of the rice, cover and cook for 5 minutes or until the spinach has wilted, the rice is tender and the stock has been absorbed. Remove from the heat and leave to stand, without lifting the lid, for 5 minutes.

Add most of the mint, check the seasoning and stir everything together. Scatter over the remaining mint and serve straight away.

If you can't get fresh apricots, use 411g can apricots in natural juice, drained and cut into wedges (adds ½ Syn per serving).

greek lamb with orzo

Filling orzo pasta and the scent of cinnamon make this sensational lamb stew a gift from the Greek gods!

serves 4

Free

ready in 1 hour

Spray a large non-stick casserole pan or saucepan with low-calorie cooking spray and place over a high heat. Add the lamb and cook for about 5 minutes or until lightly browned all over. Transfer to a plate with a slotted spoon.

Add the onions, red peppers, garlic, oregano and 3 tbsp water to the pan. Reduce the heat to medium, cover and cook for 5 minutes or until tender, then uncover, stir and cook for a few more minutes or until the excess water has gone and the onions are lightly browned. Stir in the lamb, cinnamon sticks, passata, tomato purée, carrots, celery, stock, ½ tsp salt and some black pepper. Bring to a simmer, cover and cook gently for 25 minutes.

Stir in the orzo, cover again and simmer for 15 minutes or until the orzo is tender, stirring halfway. Discard the cinnamon sticks, sprinkle with parsley and serve hot.

Crumble 75g reduced-fat feta over the stew for an indulgent topping (adds 1½ Syns per serving).

low-calorie cooking spray

600g lean lamb leg steaks, visible fat removed, cut into bite-size chunks

2 large onions, sliced

2 large red peppers, deseeded and chopped

2 garlic cloves, crushed

2 tsp dried oregano

2 small cinnamon sticks

500g passata

2 tbsp tomato purée

2 carrots, peeled and roughly chopped

2 celery sticks, sliced

600ml boiling lamb or chicken stock

300g dried orzo pasta (or another tiny pasta shape)

chopped fresh parsley, to serve

captain's chicken curry

serves 4

Free

ready in 50 minutes

400ml boiling chicken stock

2 small cinnamon sticks

½ level tsp sweetener granules

8 skinless and boneless chicken thighs, cut into chunky strips

300g green beans, trimmed, each cut into 3 pieces

2 large carrots, peeled and roughly chopped

1 tbsp lime juice

½ small pack fresh coriander, chopped

for the curry paste

2 red chillies, deseeded and roughly chopped

½ tsp chilli powder

250g shallots, chopped

2 tsp Chinese five-spice powder

2 tsp turmeric

6 garlic cloves, peeled

50g piece fresh root ginger, peeled and roughly chopped

2 lemongrass stalks, outer leaves discarded, roughly chopped

They'll all be saluting you when you serve up this Free favourite from Malaysia! Also known as a kapitan curry, it combines elements of both Indian and Chinese cuisine.

Put all the curry paste ingredients into a food processor, add 3 tbsp water and blend to a smooth curry paste.

Place a large non-stick saucepan over a low heat, add your curry paste and 3 tbsp stock and fry gently for 5 minutes or until aromatic.

Add the rest of the stock plus the cinnamon sticks, sweetener, chicken, green beans, carrots and some seasoning. Bring to the boil over a high heat then reduce the heat to low and simmer for 30 minutes or until the chicken and vegetables are tender and the sauce has reduced and thickened.

Stir in the lime juice and most of the coriander and check the seasoning. Scatter over the remaining coriander to serve. This is delicious with rice – or plain cauliflower rice if you want to keep it suitable for Extra Easy *SP*.

Add 100ml coconut milk with the chicken for a creamier captain's curry (adds 1 Syn per serving).

chinese chicken rice

Make special fried rice even more special with this Free oven-baked version of the takeaway classic.

Preheat your oven to 180°C/fan 160°C/gas 4.

Put the oyster sauce, soy sauce, sweetener, garlic, ginger, chilli and five-spice powder in a bowl and mix well. Add the chicken and toss to coat well.

Place a large non-stick casserole pan over a medium heat. Remove the chicken thighs from the marinade, shaking off any excess and reserving the remaining marinade. Add the chicken thighs to the pan and fry for 2 minutes on each side or until lightly browned. Transfer to a plate and set aside.

Add the onion, peppers and 3 tbsp water to the pan, cover and cook over a low heat for 10 minutes or until tender. Uncover, increase the heat slightly and cook until the excess water has evaporated and the onions are lightly golden.

Stir the rice, stock, half the spring onions and the remaining marinade into the vegetables. Return the chicken thighs to the pan and shake it slightly so that they settle down into the mixture, then cover and bring to a simmer. Transfer the pan to the oven and cook for 35-40 minutes or until the chicken and rice are cooked.

Remove the pan from the oven, stand for 5 minutes and scatter over the remaining spring onions to serve.

serves 4

Free

ready in 1 hour, plus standing

---

3 tbsp oyster sauce

1 tbsp dark soy sauce

1 level tsp sweetener granules

3 garlic cloves, crushed

3cm piece fresh root ginger, peeled and grated

1 red chilli, deseeded and finely chopped

1 tsp Chinese five-spice powder

8 large skinless and boneless chicken thighs

1 medium onion, chopped

2 red peppers, deseeded and roughly chopped

2 yellow peppers, deseeded and roughly chopped

350g dried brown basmati and wild rice or dried brown basmati rice

800ml boiling chicken stock

8 spring onions, thinly sliced on the diagonal

tomato soup
with turkey meatballs

serves 4

1 Syn per serving

ready in 50 minutes

500g lean turkey mince
(5% fat or less)

½ small pack fresh basil, finely
chopped, plus leaves to serve

1 tsp dried oregano

3 level tbsp freshly grated
Parmesan cheese,
plus 1 level tbsp to serve

low-calorie cooking spray

1 large onion, finely chopped

2 garlic cloves, crushed

2 tbsp tomato purée

2 x 400g cans chopped
tomatoes with herbs

750ml boiling chicken stock

100g dried linguine or spaghetti,
broken into 5cm lengths

This clever low-Syn recipe brings together soothing tomato soup and satisfying pasta and meatballs. It's not quite how Mamma used to make it… but it's how she'll make it in future!

Put the turkey, basil, oregano, Parmesan, ½ tsp salt and some black pepper in a large bowl and mix well with clean hands. Shape the mixture into about 36 little meatballs.

Spray a large non-stick saucepan with low-calorie cooking spray and place over a medium-high heat. Add half the meatballs and fry for 2-3 minutes, turning them as they brown. Transfer to a plate and repeat with the remaining meatballs.

Add the onion and garlic to the pan along with 3 tbsp water. Cover and cook over a low heat for 10 minutes or until the onion is soft. Uncover the pan and stir in the tomato purée, chopped tomatoes and stock. Bring to the boil over a high heat then reduce the heat to low and simmer for 10 minutes. (If you prefer a smooth soup, purée with a stick blender or use a liquidiser and return to the pan.)

Add the linguine or spaghetti and simmer for 10 minutes. Add the meatballs and simmer for 5 minutes or until the meatballs and linguine or spaghetti are cooked through. Season to taste.

Ladle the soup and meatballs into bowls, scatter over the basil leaves and remaining Parmesan and serve hot.

thai red duck and aubergine curry

serves 4

2 Syns per serving

ready in 40 minutes

200ml reduced-fat coconut milk

150ml boiling chicken stock

2 large potatoes, peeled and cut into small chunks

1 large aubergine, cut into small chunks

2 large duck breasts (about 400g), skinned, visible fat removed, thinly sliced

300g cherry tomatoes

1 tbsp Thai fish sauce (nam pla)

1 tbsp lime juice, plus wedges to serve

fresh basil leaves, to serve

for the curry paste

2 medium-hot red chillies, deseeded and chopped

75g shallots, roughly chopped

2 lemongrass stalks, outer leaves discarded, chopped

5cm piece fresh root ginger, peeled and chopped

4 garlic cloves, peeled

1 tsp fennel seeds, crushed

1 tbsp ground coriander

2 tsp ground cumin

¼ tsp ground nutmeg

We've made our own tastebud-tingling curry paste to keep the Syns in this must-try Thai curry as low as possible.

Put all the curry paste ingredients in a food processor, add ¼ tsp freshly ground black pepper and 3 tbsp water and blend until smooth.

Place a large non-stick saucepan over a medium-low heat. Add your curry paste and 3 tbsp coconut milk and fry gently for 5 minutes or until fragrant. Add the remaining coconut milk and the stock and bring to a simmer.

Add the potatoes and aubergine to the pan and simmer for 15 minutes or until the potatoes are just tender. Add the duck and tomatoes, bring back to a simmer and cook for 5 minutes or until the duck is tender and the sauce has reduced slightly.

Stir in the Thai fish sauce and lime juice and check the seasoning. Scatter over the basil leaves and serve hot with lime wedges.

spanish-style fish stew

Seafood plays a big part in Spain's cuisine, and this simple Free stew packed with filling Speed veggies is a perfect example.

Place a large non-stick casserole pan over a medium-low heat. Add the onions, red peppers, carrots, fennel, chilli flakes, garlic, fennel seeds, 4 tbsp stock, ½ tsp salt and some black pepper. Cover and cook for 5 minutes or until beginning to soften.

Add the saffron or turmeric, paprika, tomatoes, potatoes and remaining stock. Bring to a gentle simmer and cook uncovered for 20 minutes or until the potatoes are tender.

Add the celery and simmer for 2 minutes, then stir in the lemon juice, scatter the fish and prawns on top and season lightly. Cover the pan and simmer gently for 5 minutes or until the fish and prawns are just cooked through. Scatter over the parsley to serve.

serves 4

Free

ready in 50 minutes

---

2 medium onions, halved and sliced

2 red peppers, deseeded and roughly chopped

2 carrots, peeled and roughly chopped

1 fennel bulb, sliced

1 tsp dried chilli flakes

2 garlic cloves, crushed

1 tsp fennel seeds, lightly crushed

500ml boiling fish or vegetable stock

pinch of saffron or ½ tsp turmeric

2 tsp smoked paprika

2 x 400g cans chopped tomatoes

2 large potatoes, peeled and cut into small chunks

2 celery sticks, sliced

1 tbsp lemon juice

400g skinless and boneless white fish fillets, cut into bite-size chunks

200g raw peeled king or tiger prawns, with or without tails

chopped fresh parsley, to serve

mildly curried
mussel chowder

serves 4

2 Syns per serving

ready in 30 minutes

Chowders are soups made with milk and this mouth-watering meal uses coconut milk for an appealing Asian flavour.

1kg fresh mussels

500g potatoes, peeled and diced

¾ tsp turmeric

1 medium onion, chopped

1 leek, sliced

1 red pepper, deseeded and roughly chopped

4 back bacon rashers, visible fat removed, finely chopped

2 garlic cloves, crushed

500ml boiling chicken or vegetable stock

1 tbsp mild curry powder

200ml reduced-fat coconut milk

2 tomatoes, deseeded and finely chopped

½ small pack fresh coriander, chopped

First prepare the mussels. Tip them into the sink and wash under cold running water, discarding any that won't close when tapped or that have broken shells. Pull out and discard any wispy 'beards' from between the closed shells.

Bring a large casserole pan or saucepan of water to the boil over a high heat. Add the potatoes and ¼ tsp turmeric, bring back to the boil and simmer for about 7-8 minutes or until tender but not falling apart. Drain and set aside.

Return the pan to a low heat and add the onion, leek, red pepper, bacon, garlic and 4 tbsp stock. Cover and cook over a low heat for 10 minutes or until the onion and pepper are soft.

Uncover the pan, increase the heat to high and stir in the curry powder and remaining turmeric. Cook for 1 minute. Add the mussels and remaining stock, cover and cook for 3 minutes or until the mussels have opened, discarding any that stay closed.

Stir in the coconut milk and bring back to a gentle simmer. Stir in the tomatoes, cooked potatoes, three-quarters of the coriander and some seasoning to taste. Serve in shallow bowls, with the remaining coriander sprinkled over.

hot and sour squid soup

Asian food fans will love this beautifully balanced soup, with the fantastic texture and subtle flavour of squid stealing the show!

Bring the stock, sweetener and kaffir lime leaves to a simmer in a large saucepan over a medium heat.

Put all the garlic paste ingredients in a small food processor, add 3 tbsp water and blend to a paste. Add to the stock and simmer for 2 minutes, then add the fish sauce, soy sauce, tamarind and lime juice and simmer for 1 minute more.

Add the sweetcorn to the pan and simmer for 2 minutes, then add the rest of the vegetables and the squid, bring back to the boil and simmer for 1 minute. (Take care not to cook any longer or the squid will become tough.)

Ladle the soup into bowls, scatter with the extra chilli and spring onions and serve hot.

Use large raw peeled prawns instead of squid if you like, cooking them until they turn pink.

serves 4

Free

ready in 25 minutes

1.2 litres boiling chicken stock

½ level tsp sweetener granules

2 fresh or dried kaffir lime leaves

4 tbsp Thai fish sauce (nam pla)

1 tbsp light soy sauce

½ level tsp tamarind paste

3 tbsp lime juice

175g baby sweetcorn, halved lengthways

250g oyster mushrooms, thickly sliced

2 tomatoes, roughly chopped

3 spring onions, thinly sliced on the diagonal, plus extra to serve

100g baby leaf spinach

400g prepared squid rings, thawed if frozen

for the garlic paste

6 garlic cloves, peeled

5cm piece fresh root ginger, peeled and roughly chopped

2 lemongrass stalks, outer leaves discarded, roughly chopped

2 medium-hot red chillies, deseeded, plus extra to serve

prawn, coconut and okra curry

serves 4

2 Syns per serving

ready in 50 minutes

Okra is a hidden gem of a Speed vegetable, although it's widely available in supermarkets and works brilliantly in many curries and stews.

400g raw peeled king or tiger prawns

1 tsp turmeric

1 tsp cumin seeds

200ml reduced-fat coconut milk

200g chopped tomatoes

200ml boiling chicken stock

12 curry leaves (optional)

1 medium-hot green chilli, deseeded and thinly sliced

175g okra, halved lengthways

1 tbsp garam masala

½ level tsp sweetener granules

1 tbsp lime juice

3 tbsp fat-free natural Greek yogurt

chopped fresh coriander, to serve

for the curry paste

300g shallots, roughly chopped

5cm piece fresh root ginger, peeled and roughly chopped

6 garlic cloves, peeled

½ tsp chilli powder

½ tsp paprika

Put the prawns in a bowl with the turmeric and a little salt, toss well and set aside.

Put the curry paste ingredients into a small food processor with 2 tbsp water and blend to a smooth paste.

Place a non-stick saucepan or casserole pan over a medium-high heat. Add your curry paste, the cumin seeds and 2 tbsp coconut milk and cook gently, stirring, for 5 minutes or until aromatic.

Stir in the remaining coconut milk along with the tomatoes, stock, curry leaves, if using, green chilli and okra and simmer gently for 30 minutes.

Stir in the prawns, garam masala and sweetener and simmer for 5 minutes or until the prawns have turned pink and are just cooked through. Remove from the heat and stir in the lime juice and yogurt. Check the seasoning and scatter over the coriander to serve.

serves 4

Free

v

ready in 50 minutes, plus standing

---

large pinch of saffron or 1 tsp turmeric

750ml boiling vegetable stock

low-calorie cooking spray

350g Quorn Chicken-style Pieces

1 tbsp fresh thyme leaves

grated zest of ½ small unwaxed lemon

1 large onion, chopped

3 garlic cloves, crushed

1 large red pepper, deseeded and thickly sliced

1 large yellow pepper, deseeded and thickly sliced

200g green beans, trimmed and cut into short pieces

2 tsp smoked paprika

227g can chopped tomatoes

350g dried paella rice

400g can artichoke hearts in water, drained and quartered

quorn paella

A plateful of paella is great warm weather food, and we've packed this easy oven-baked version with chunks of Quorn and a host of vibrant veggies.

Preheat your oven to 180°C/fan 160°C/gas 4.

Put the saffron or turmeric and stock in a heatproof jug, stir and set aside.

Spray a non-stick paella pan or casserole pan with low-calorie cooking spray and place over a medium heat. Add the Quorn and fry gently until golden brown all over. Transfer to a bowl and add 1 tsp thyme leaves, the lemon zest and some seasoning. Mix well.

Add the onion, garlic, peppers, remaining thyme, 3 tbsp water and some seasoning to the pan. Cover, reduce the heat to low and cook for 10 minutes or until soft. Add the green beans, cover again and cook for 5 minutes.

Uncover the pan, stir in the smoked paprika, tomatoes, rice, stock and ½ tsp salt and bring to a simmer, stirring once to make sure the rice doesn't stick to the pan. Scatter the Quorn and artichokes on top and shake the pan gently so that they sink down into the mixture a little. Cover the pan again and cook in the oven for 20 minutes, by which time all the liquid should have been absorbed and the rice should be tender.

Remove from the oven and leave to stand, still covered, for a further 5 minutes. Serve hot.

one for all | **pot luck**

mushroom macaroni

serves 4

Free

ready in 20 minutes, plus soaking

30g dried porcini mushrooms

low-calorie cooking spray

400g mini portobello or chestnut
mushrooms, sliced

3 garlic cloves, crushed

2 tsp fresh thyme leaves

500g dried macaroni

1 litre boiling vegetable stock

200g plain quark

3 tbsp chopped fresh parsley

Pasta ticks all the boxes when you need fast, filling food. This easy recipe partners macaroni with savoury mushrooms coated in creamy quark. And best of all, it's Free!

Put the porcini mushrooms in a heatproof bowl, cover with boiling water and leave to soak for at least 20 minutes. Drain and finely chop, discarding the soaking liquid.

Spray a large non-stick saucepan with low-calorie cooking spray and place over a medium-high heat. Add the porcini mushrooms, fresh mushrooms, garlic and thyme and cook until the juices start to run from the mushrooms. Increase the heat to high and stir-fry for 5 minutes or until the mushrooms are tender.

Add the macaroni, stock and a little salt and pepper and bring to the boil, stirring to make sure nothing sticks. Cover and simmer for 10-12 minutes or until the macaroni is just tender and nearly all the stock has been absorbed, giving everything a stir now and then.

Remove from the heat and stir in the quark and most of the parsley. Check the seasoning and sprinkle with the remaining parsley to serve.

For an extra touch of luxury, scatter over freshly grated Parmesan cheese or a vegetarian alternative (adds 1 Syn per level tbsp).

kichiri with cabbage and eggs

This spicy rice dish is a much-loved comfort food in India – in fact it's part of kedgeree's family tree, without the fish!

serves 4

Free

ready in 35 minutes

Bring some water to the boil in a large non-stick casserole pan over a high heat. Add the eggs and boil for 7 minutes then drain and set aside.

Spray the pan with low-calorie cooking spray and add the cumin seeds, cabbage, ½ tsp turmeric and a good pinch of salt. Stir-fry for 1½-2 minutes or until just tender then tip on to a plate and set aside.

Spray the pan with a little more low-calorie cooking spray and add the ginger, chilli, cinnamon, cardamom, cloves, curry leaves, if using, the remaining turmeric and 2 tbsp water. Stir-fry for 2-3 minutes or until the water has evaporated and the mixture is fragrant. Stir in the rice, lentils and stock and bring to the boil. Stir once and cover, then reduce the heat to low and cook for 12 minutes.

Remove the pan from the heat and stir in the garam masala, cabbage and most of the spring onions. Cover again and leave to rest for 5 minutes.

Meanwhile, peel and halve the eggs.

Spoon the rice on to plates and top with the eggs and remaining spring onions. Delicious with garlic yogurt (see tip).

To make a Free garlic yogurt to serve with this, mix 150g fat-free natural Greek yogurt, 2 crushed garlic cloves, ¼ tsp paprika and a pinch or 2 of sweetener and salt.

6 large eggs*

low-calorie cooking spray

1 tsp cumin seeds

1 small pointed spring cabbage, cored, leaves shredded

1 tsp turmeric

3cm piece fresh root ginger, peeled and grated

1 medium-hot red chilli, deseeded and finely chopped

1 small cinnamon stick, halved

8 green cardamom pods, cracked open

6 cloves

12 curry leaves (optional)

250g dried basmati rice

400g can green lentils, drained and rinsed

450ml boiling vegetable stock

1 tsp garam masala

8 spring onions, thinly sliced

Pregnant women, the elderly, babies and toddlers are advised to choose eggs showing the British Lion stamp if eating raw or partially cooked eggs.

harissa-spiced quinoa with carrots

serves 4

Free

🅥 **vegan**

ready in 30 minutes

2 large courgettes, diced

200g sugar snap peas or mangetout, shredded

1 tsp cumin seeds

2 large carrots, peeled and coarsely grated

250g dried quinoa

500ml boiling vegetable stock

1 level tsp chilli paste

1 tsp harissa spice

400g can chickpeas, drained and rinsed

2 tbsp lemon juice

The chewy texture of quinoa makes a fantastic base for this warm salad, giving other ingredients the chance to shine!

Place a large non-stick saucepan over a medium heat. Add the courgettes, sugar snaps or mangetout, cumin seeds and 2-3 tbsp water and stir-fry for 2 minutes. Add the carrots and continue to stir-fry for 1-2 minutes or until the vegetables are just tender. Scoop on to a plate and set aside. Wipe the pan.

Put the quinoa in a sieve and rinse under cold running water, rubbing the grains with your fingers. Shake away the excess water, tip into the frying pan and increase the heat to medium-high. Stir-fry for 3-4 minutes or until dry and starting to smell slightly nutty.

Add the stock, chilli paste, harissa spice and chickpeas to the quinoa and bring to the boil. Reduce the heat to low, cover and simmer for 15 minutes or until all the liquid has been absorbed and the quinoa is tender – it's done when the little curled strands pop out from the grains (you might need to top up with a little more stock or water if the quinoa looks dry).

Uncover the quinoa and fluff up the grains with a fork, then add the lemon juice and stir-fried vegetables. Mix together gently, heat through and serve hot.

courgette and tomato risotto

Risottos are a timeless way to make a meal out of a few simple ingredients, with rice and stock combining brilliantly with just about anything you care to add.

Place a deep non-stick casserole pan or saucepan over a low heat. Add the onion, chilli flakes and 2 tbsp water, cover and cook for 5 minutes or until just soft.

Increase the heat to medium, add the courgettes and cook for 5 minutes, stirring. Stir in the rice and a good splash of the hot stock, bring to a simmer and stir until all the stock has been absorbed before adding another good splash of stock. Continue like this for about 25 minutes, stirring frequently. You might not need to use all of the stock.

About 5 minutes before the end of the cooking time, stir in the cherry tomatoes, lemon zest and spinach and cook until the rice is creamy and tender but still has a little bit of bite.

Season to taste, scatter over the basil leaves and serve hot.

serves 4

Free

 vegan

ready in 35 minutes

---

1 medium red onion, finely chopped

¼ tsp dried chilli flakes

200g baby or small courgettes, sliced

300g dried risotto rice

1 litre boiling vegetable stock

200g cherry tomatoes, quartered

grated zest of ½ small unwaxed lemon

100g frozen spinach, thawed

fresh basil leaves, to serve

that fry-day feeling

Serve up sizzling Free and low-Syn suppers cooked in frying pans and woks, such as honey & saffron chicken, Malay tofu noodles and a pizza omelette.

braised steak and mushrooms

serves 4

1 Syn per serving

ready in 3 hours

---

4 thick-cut lean braising steaks, visible fat removed

2 level tbsp plain flour

low-calorie cooking spray

3 medium onions, halved and sliced

1 level tsp sweetener granules

6 garlic cloves, crushed

½ tsp dried mixed herbs

700ml boiling beef stock, made using 3 tbsp beef liquid stock concentrate

3 tbsp Worcestershire sauce

800g mushrooms, peeled and thickly sliced

chopped fresh parsley, to serve

Meat-lovers will adore these tender beef steaks and vegetables simmered in a deeply savoury sauce.

Season the steaks on both sides, dust in the flour and set aside.

Spray a deep, lidded non-stick frying pan with low-calorie cooking spray and place over a low heat. Add the onions and 3 tbsp water, cover and cook for 10 minutes or until soft.

Uncover the pan, add the sweetener and increase the heat to high. Cook for another 10 minutes or until the onions are nicely browned and caramelised, stirring frequently.

Stir in the garlic, mixed herbs, stock and Worcestershire sauce. Add the steaks to the pan along with the mushrooms, cover and bring to a simmer. Reduce the heat to low and cook gently for 1½ hours.

Uncover the pan and simmer gently for another 1 hour or until the sauce has reduced and thickened and the steaks are meltingly tender. Scatter over the parsley to serve. This is delicious with mashed potatoes – or swede mash if you want to keep it suitable for Extra Easy *SP*.

creole beef stir-fry

This quick and easy beef and bacon stir-fry is inspired by Creole cuisine, which comes from the southern US state of Louisiana and has its roots in the food of Spain and France.

Spray a deep, non-stick frying pan or wok with low-calorie cooking spray and place over a high heat. Add the beef, bacon, garlic, chilli powder, cumin and sweetener and stir-fry for 2-3 minutes or until the beef is nicely browned, breaking up any lumps of beef with a wooden spoon.

Drain off any fat in the pan, add the cabbage and stir-fry for a further 3-4 minutes or until just tender.

Add the sweetcorn, tomatoes and spring onions and stir-fry for 2-3 minutes or until the sweetcorn has heated through and any liquid has gone. Season to taste with salt, top with a few jalapeño chilli slices and serve with more jalapeños on the side for those who can handle the heat!

serves 4

Free

ready in 20 minutes

---

low-calorie cooking spray

500g lean beef mince (5% fat or less)

4 back bacon rashers, visible fat removed, cut into thin strips

3 garlic cloves, crushed

1 tbsp chilli powder

1 tsp ground cumin

¼ level tsp sweetener granules

½ Savoy cabbage, cored, thick ribs discarded, leaves shredded

340g can sweetcorn kernels in water, drained

3 tomatoes, diced

8 spring onions, thinly sliced

sliced jalapeño chillies from a jar, drained, to serve

swedish pork meatballs

serves 4

Free

ready in 35 minutes

Enjoy the fun and flavour of Swedish meatballs without the Syns… or the flat-packed furniture!

750g lean pork mince (5% fat or less)

1 small onion, finely chopped

1 large garlic clove, crushed

¼ tsp freshly grated nutmeg

½ small pack fresh dill, chopped

1 medium egg, beaten

low-calorie cooking spray

300ml boiling chicken stock

1 tsp chopped fresh rosemary

1 tsp tomato purée

2 tsp Worcestershire sauce

1 tsp dark soy sauce

1 level tsp cornflour

150g plain quark (see tip)

2 tbsp fat-free natural Greek yogurt (see tip)

½ tsp paprika

Put the pork, onion, garlic, nutmeg, 2 tbsp dill, egg, ¾ tsp salt and ½ tsp black pepper in a mixing bowl and mix well. Shape the mixture into 28 meatballs, each about the size of a golf ball.

Spray a large non-stick frying pan with low-calorie cooking spray and place over a medium-high heat. Add the meatballs and fry for 8 minutes or until well browned all over and cooked through (you might need to do this in batches). Lift the meatballs on to a plate, cover with foil and keep warm.

Add the stock, rosemary and tomato purée to the pan and bring to a simmer. Add the Worcestershire sauce, soy sauce and some seasoning to taste, then return the meatballs to the pan. Reduce the heat to low and simmer gently until they have heated through.

Mix the cornflour with 6 tbsp quark and add to the pan, swirling it until the sauce is gently simmering and has slightly thickened.

To make some quark 'soured cream', mix the remaining quark with the yogurt, paprika, 1 tbsp dill and some seasoning to taste.

Scatter the remaining dill over the meatballs and serve with the quark 'soured cream'. This is fantastic with tagliatelle pasta and green Speed vegetables.

Get your quark and yogurt out of the fridge when you start cooking so that they aren't too cold when you add them to the pan. This can help reduce the risk of them splitting.

one for all | **that fry-day feeling**

serves 4

1 Syn per serving

ready in 25 minutes

150g green beans, trimmed

1 tbsp curry powder
(heat to your taste)

1 tsp ground coriander

1 tsp chilli powder

½ tsp turmeric

6 garlic cloves, crushed

3cm piece fresh root ginger,
peeled and grated

600g lean lamb leg steaks,
visible fat removed, thinly sliced

low-calorie cooking spray

2 small red onions,
halved and sliced

2 small sweet peppers
(any colours), deseeded and
sliced (or use regular peppers)

12 curry leaves (optional)

½ tsp fennel seeds or cumin
seeds, lightly crushed

100ml reduced-fat coconut milk

2 tbsp lime juice

sri lankan lamb with sweet peppers

Luxurious lamb and creamy coconut milk turn this beautifully spiced stir-fry curry into something extra special.

Bring some water to the boil in a large, deep non-stick frying pan or wok over a high heat. Add the green beans, bring back to the boil and cook for 2 minutes. Drain well and set aside on a plate.

Meanwhile, mix the spices, garlic, ginger, ½ tsp black pepper and ½ tsp salt in a bowl. Add the lamb and stir to coat well.

Spray the pan with low-calorie cooking spray and place over a high heat. Add the onions and peppers, stir-fry for 5 minutes and transfer to the plate with the green beans.

Add the lamb to the pan along with the curry leaves, if using, fennel seeds or cumin seeds and 3 tbsp water. Stir-fry for 3 minutes or until the lamb is just cooked through.

Return the green beans, onions and peppers to the pan, add the coconut milk and stir-fry for 1 minute. Stir in the lime juice to serve.

chicken mole

serves 4

1 Syn per serving

ready in 50 minutes

---

low-calorie cooking spray

4 large skinless and boneless chicken breasts

1 large onion, roughly chopped

2 celery sticks, roughly chopped

2 garlic cloves, crushed

1 tbsp ground coriander

1 tsp chilli powder

½ tsp ground cinnamon

500g passata

100ml boiling chicken stock

1 tsp dried oregano

1 tsp Tabasco sauce (chipotle flavour if possible)

400g can red kidney beans, drained and rinsed

15g plain dark chocolate, grated

fresh coriander sprigs, to serve

A little bit of chocolate (yes, chocolate!) gives this spicy Mexican dish an authentic and delicious finish.

Spray a deep, lidded non-stick frying pan with low-calorie cooking spray and place over a high heat. Season the chicken breasts, add them to the pan and brown for a few minutes on each side. Set aside on a plate.

Add the onion, celery, garlic and 3 tbsp water to the pan. Cover and cook over a low heat for 10 minutes or until soft. Uncover the pan and stir in the spices, passata, stock, oregano and Tabasco. Simmer for 15 minutes or until the sauce has reduced and thickened.

Blitz with a stick blender (or use a food processor and return the sauce to the pan). Add the chicken breasts and kidney beans to the sauce, part-cover and simmer for 15 minutes or until the chicken is cooked through. Season to taste.

Add the chocolate to the sauce, stir until melted and scatter over the coriander sprigs to serve. This is great with rice and Speed vegetables.

honey and saffron chicken

There's a lovely warmth to this low-Syn North African-style chicken dish thanks to the fresh ginger and a host of sensational spices.

serves 4

½ **Syn** per serving

❄ (without the couscous)

ready in 50 minutes

Spray a deep, lidded non-stick frying pan with low-calorie cooking spray and place over a medium heat. Add the chicken thighs, fry until nicely browned on both sides then lift on to a plate and set aside.

Add the onion and 2 tbsp water to the pan and reduce the heat to low. Cover and cook for 10 minutes or until soft.

Uncover the pan and stir in the garlic, fresh ginger, chilli paste, cinnamon stick, ground ginger, harissa, tomatoes, stock, saffron and a little seasoning. Return the chicken to the pan, increase the heat to high and bring to the boil. Reduce the heat to low and simmer gently for 30 minutes or until the chicken is tender and the sauce has reduced and thickened.

About 10 minutes before the chicken is ready, put the couscous into a heatproof bowl. Mix the chicken liquid stock concentrate with 375ml boiling water, pour over the couscous and cover with cling film. Leave for 5-10 minutes then fluff up the grains with a fork and stir in the lemon zest.

Add the lemon juice and honey to the chicken, simmer for 2 minutes and check the seasoning. Scatter the mint over the chicken and couscous and serve hot with salad leaves.

low-calorie cooking spray

8 large skinless and boneless chicken thighs

1 large onion, chopped

3 garlic cloves, crushed

5cm piece fresh root ginger, peeled and finely grated

½ level tsp chilli paste

1 small cinnamon stick

1 tsp ground ginger

1 tsp harissa spice

2 x 400g cans chopped tomatoes

300ml boiling chicken stock

½ tsp saffron

300g dried couscous

2 tsp chicken liquid stock concentrate

grated zest of 1 small unwaxed lemon, plus 2 tbsp juice

1 level tbsp runny honey

roughly chopped fresh mint, to serve

coq au vin

serves 4

1½ Syns per serving

ready in 45 minutes

---

low-calorie cooking spray

400g small shallots, peeled

8 skinless and boneless chicken thighs, halved

4 back bacon rashers, visible fat removed, cut into strips

120ml medium-strength red wine

2 tbsp tomato purée

200ml boiling chicken stock

2 garlic cloves, crushed

200g small carrots, peeled and thinly sliced on the diagonal

200g button mushrooms, halved or quartered

200g cherry tomatoes, halved

1 tbsp fresh thyme leaves

1 level tbsp cornflour

chopped fresh parsley, to serve

A small glass of wine goes a long way in this super-simple version of the classic French recipe.

Spray a large, lidded non-stick frying pan with low-calorie cooking spray and place over a medium heat. Add the shallots and cook for about 5 minutes or until golden brown all over, turning regularly.

Add the chicken and bacon, increase the heat slightly and fry for 7-8 minutes or until the chicken is golden brown.

Add the wine to the pan and simmer rapidly until it has reduced by half. Stir in the tomato purée, stock, garlic, carrots, mushrooms, tomatoes, thyme and some salt and pepper. Cover and simmer for 10 minutes, then uncover the pan and simmer for a further 10 minutes or until the sauce has reduced slightly and the chicken is cooked.

Mix the cornflour with a little water, stir it into the sauce and simmer for 1 minute or until thickened. Scatter over the parsley to serve.

sicilian tuna with salsa

Pan-frying is ideal for fresh tuna steaks and our punchy salsa is the perfect partner.

First make the salsa by putting the tomatoes, red onion, spring onions, capers, chilli, 1 tbsp lemon juice and most of the parsley in a bowl. Mix well and season to taste.

Put the rest of the lemon juice in a shallow dish with the garlic, dried and fresh oregano, remaining chopped parsley and some black pepper. Add the tuna steaks, turn to coat well and sprinkle lightly with a little salt.

Spray a large non-stick griddle pan or frying pan with a little low-calorie cooking spray and place over a high heat. Add the tuna steaks and cook for 1½-2 minutes on each side or until browned on the outside but pink and juicy in the centre (or cook for longer if you prefer).

Put the tuna steaks and salsa on to plates and sprinkle with the extra parsley and oregano to serve.

serves 4

Free

ready in 15 minutes

300g cherry tomatoes, quartered

1 small red onion, finely chopped

4 spring onions, thinly sliced

2 tbsp capers, drained and rinsed

½ medium-hot red chilli, deseeded and finely chopped

juice of 1 lemon

2 tbsp chopped fresh parsley, plus extra to serve

1 large garlic clove, crushed

1 tsp dried oregano

1 tbsp chopped fresh oregano, plus extra to serve

4 large or 8 small tuna steaks, each about 2.5cm thick

low-calorie cooking spray

seafood sizzle
with salsa verde

serves 4

Free

ready in 15 minutes

---

low-calorie cooking spray

400g raw peeled king or tiger prawns

400g skinless and boneless firm white fish fillets, cut across into bite-size chunks

8 prepared scallops, with the orange coral left on if you like

pinch of paprika

1 small cucumber

small bag of rocket leaves

for the salsa verde

½ small pack fresh parsley, finely chopped, plus extra to serve

1 tbsp finely chopped fresh mint

1½ tbsp capers, drained, rinsed and finely chopped

1 garlic clove, crushed

¼ tsp mustard powder

2 tbsp lemon juice

1 tbsp white wine vinegar

Dive in to this delicious deep-sea platter, served with a vibrant salsa verde.

First put all the salsa verde ingredients in a small bowl, add 1 tbsp cold water and ¼ tsp salt and mix well. Set aside.

Spray a large non-stick frying pan with low-calorie cooking spray and place over a high heat. When hot, add the prawns, season lightly and sizzle for 1 minute on each side or until pink and cooked through. Lift on to a plate, cover to keep hot and set aside.

Add the fish chunks and scallops to the pan, season lightly, sprinkle with the paprika and spray with a little more low-calorie cooking spray. Sizzle for 1½ minutes on each side or until just cooked through. Add to the prawns and keep hot.

Peel the cucumber into ribbons with a vegetable peeler and spread out on a serving platter along with the rocket. Arrange the prawns, fish and scallops on top, scatter over the extra parsley and serve with the salsa verde.

mackerel with rainbow pickles

serves 4

Free

ready in 20 minutes

1 large fennel bulb, thinly sliced

150g radishes, thinly sliced

200g sugar snap peas or mangetout, sliced lengthways

1 large carrot, peeled and shredded or grated

1 medium red onion, halved and thinly sliced

150ml white wine vinegar

3 level tbsp sweetener granules

1 tsp yellow mustard seeds

low-calorie cooking spray

8 fresh boneless mackerel fillets

Fresh mackerel is so good for you and looks simply spectacular on a bed of brightly coloured pickles.

Put the fennel, radishes, sugar snaps or mangetout, carrot and red onion in a large heatproof bowl and toss together.

Put the vinegar, sweetener, mustard seeds, 100ml water and ¼ tsp freshly ground black pepper in a non-stick frying pan and bring to the boil over a high heat. Pour the mixture over the vegetables and set aside, turning them over now and again when you cook the mackerel.

Wipe the pan, spray with low-calorie cooking spray and place over a medium-high heat. Season the mackerel fillets on both sides. Add 4 fillets to the pan, skin-side down, and cook for 2 minutes on each side or until cooked through. Lift on to a plate and keep warm while you cook the rest.

Drain the pickled vegetables, discarding the vinegar, and return them to the bowl. Add a pinch of salt and toss well, then divide between plates and serve with the mackerel.

cheesy cajun brunch scramble

serves 4

2 Syns per serving

ready in 20 minutes

There's so much going on in every mouthful of this spicy scramble, including a cheeky sprinkling of cheese!

low-calorie cooking spray

3 peppers (any colours), deseeded and diced

1 mild green chilli, deseeded and finely chopped

400g can or carton black beans or red kidney beans, drained and rinsed

8 spring onions, thinly sliced

12 large eggs*, beaten

few shakes of Tabasco sauce

2 tomatoes, diced

50g reduced-fat Cheddar cheese, coarsely grated

Pregnant women, the elderly, babies and toddlers are advised to choose eggs showing the British Lion stamp if eating raw or partially cooked eggs.

Spray a large, lidded non-stick frying pan with low-calorie cooking spray and place over a medium-high heat. Add the peppers and 2 tbsp water, cover and cook for 5 minutes or until just tender. Add the chilli, beans and half the spring onions, cover again and cook for 5 minutes or until the spring onions are soft and the beans have heated through. Reduce the heat to medium.

Preheat the grill to high.

Season the eggs, add them to the pan and gently scramble with a spatula until they are almost done but still moist and very slightly soft here and there. Remove the pan from the heat.

Sprinkle the Tabasco over the eggs and scatter over the tomatoes, remaining spring onions and the cheese. Finish under the grill for 2-3 minutes or until set to your liking. Serve hot with salad, if you like.

malay tofu noodles

That bottle of tomato ketchup in your storecupboard is the secret ingredient in this exotic fakeaway, which also features filling egg and tofu plus loads of tasty veggies.

Wrap the tofu in plenty of kitchen paper, sandwich between 2 boards and weigh it down with a few cans or something heavy. Leave for 20-30 minutes to firm up even more. Unwrap and cut into small chunks.

Spray a deep, lidded non-stick frying pan or wok with low-calorie cooking spray and place over a medium-high heat. When it's hot, season the beaten eggs and pour some into the centre of the pan. Let it flow out to make a saucer-sized pancake (it doesn't need to be perfectly round) and cook for 30 seconds. Flip it over and cook for a few seconds more or until firm. Lift on to a chopping board, roll up tightly and leave to cool. Repeat the process until you have used up all the egg then slice the omelettes into thin strips and set aside.

Spray the pan with more low-calorie cooking spray, add the tofu and cook, turning regularly, until golden brown all over. Set aside.

Half-fill the pan with water and bring to the boil. Add the noodles and cook according to the pack instructions, then drain and set aside.

Mix the tomato ketchup, chilli sauce and soy sauce in a small bowl.

Spray the pan with more low-calorie cooking spray, turn the heat to medium-low and add the shallots, garlic, chilli and 4 tbsp water. Cover and cook for 5 minutes or until soft then uncover the pan, increase the heat to medium-high and add the pak choi and 1 tbsp water. Stir-fry for 1 minute, then add the bean sprouts and spring onions and stir-fry for another minute.

Add the noodles, tofu and ketchup mixture to the pan and stir-fry for 2-3 minutes or until the noodles have heated through. Check the seasoning, add the omelette strips and toss one more time to mix well. Serve hot.

serves 4

1 Syn per serving

ready in 35 minutes, plus tofu pressing

400g pack firm plain/naturally smoked tofu

low-calorie cooking spray

4 medium eggs, beaten

250g dried medium egg noodles

4 level tbsp tomato ketchup

1 level tbsp hot chilli sauce

3 tbsp dark soy sauce

2 large shallots, thinly sliced

6 garlic cloves, finely chopped

1 medium-hot red chilli, deseeded and finely chopped

500g pak choi, sliced

300g fresh bean sprouts, rinsed

8 spring onions, sliced

cauliflower huevos rancheros

serves 2

2 Syns per serving

Ⓥ (if the cheese is vegetarian)

ready in 35 minutes

---

low-calorie cooking spray

3 echalion (banana) shallots, halved and thinly sliced across

4 tomatoes, chopped

1 heaped tsp harissa spice

1 tbsp tomato purée

300g small cauliflower florets

4 eggs*

45g reduced-fat feta cheese, diced

chopped fresh coriander, to serve

Pregnant women, the elderly, babies and toddlers are advised to choose eggs showing the British Lion stamp if eating raw or partially cooked eggs.

Our tasty twist on the popular Mexican brunch dish features cauliflower, North African harissa spice and Mediterranean feta cheese.

Lightly spray a large, lidded non-stick frying pan with low-calorie cooking spray and place over a medium heat. Add the shallots and fry for 6-7 minutes or until golden, stirring frequently.

Add the tomatoes and stir-fry for a few minutes, then add the harissa, tomato purée, 1 tbsp water and a little salt. Stir in the cauliflower, cover the pan and reduce the heat to low. Cook for 15 minutes or until the cauliflower is tender, stirring halfway.

Make 4 wells in the mixture, break an egg into each one and scatter over the feta. Cover and cook for a further 5 minutes or until the eggs are done to your liking. Scatter over the coriander and serve hot, with salad if you like.

Leave out the feta to make this dish Free!

pizza
omelette

The whole family will enjoy this healthy pizza-style meal – and as well as being completely Free it's ideal for Extra Easy *SP*!

Strip the leaves from the stalks of the chard or spinach and finely shred the leaves. (You can cook the stalks and use them as a vegetable with another meal.)

Spray a large, lidded, ovenproof non-stick frying pan with low-calorie cooking spray and place over a medium heat. Add the leek, garlic, 3 tbsp water and as much of the chard or spinach as you can fit in. Cover and cook until tender, stirring in another handful of chard or spinach every now and then. Tip into a colander and press out as much liquid as possible.

Crack the eggs into a large mixing bowl, season lightly and beat well. Stir in the chard or spinach, cottage cheese and all the herbs.

Preheat the oven to 180°C/fan 160°C/gas 4.

Wipe the pan, spray with more low-calorie cooking spray and return to a medium heat. Pour in the egg mixture and cook gently for 10 minutes or until the mixture is partially set. Scatter over the tomatoes, spring onions and chilli. Transfer the pan to the oven and bake for 10-15 minutes or until golden brown and firm all the way through.

Release the omelette with a spatula, turn out on to a large plate or serving board and cut into wedges. Serve hot with salad.

serves 4

Free

ready in 40 minutes

600g chard or mature spinach

low-calorie cooking spray

1 large leek, thinly sliced

4 garlic cloves, crushed

12 large eggs

120g low-fat natural cottage cheese

small pack fresh mint, chopped

small pack fresh basil, chopped

small pack fresh coriander, chopped

2 tomatoes, diced

4 spring onions, thinly sliced

1 medium-hot chilli (red or green), deseeded and sliced

go slow

Make your slow cooker sing with meals including Mexican pork pozole, Texan beef pot roast and a spinach & ricotta lasagne. For our helpful hints on successful slow cooking, see page 141.

texan beef pot roast

serves 4

½ **Syn** per serving

ready in 8 hours 15 minutes

---

2 medium red onions, roughly chopped

1kg boned and rolled topside beef joint

1 tbsp barbecue seasoning

200g passata

2 tbsp tomato purée

120ml boiling beef stock

4 garlic cloves, sliced

1 heaped tbsp fresh thyme leaves

2 large floury potatoes, peeled and cut into small chunks

3 carrots, peeled and roughly chopped

2 celery sticks, roughly chopped

2 large red peppers, deseeded and roughly chopped

1 level tbsp cornflour

chopped fresh parsley, to serve

Our all-American meat feast comes with delicious chunks of veg and an irresistible barbecue-style sauce!

Put the onions in the slow cooker pot. Pull the string off the beef joint, trim off and discard any visible fat, then re-position the strings to keep the joint in a neat shape. Season the beef with the barbecue seasoning, ½ tsp salt and some pepper and place it on top of the onions.

Mix the passata with the tomato purée, stock, garlic and thyme and pour it over the beef. Cover and cook on low for 4 hours.

Transfer the beef to a plate and stir the potatoes, carrots, celery and peppers into the sauce in the slow cooker pot. Return the beef to the pot and push it down as far as you can into the vegetables, making sure the potatoes and carrots are covered with the liquid. Cover again and cook for another 4-6 hours or until the beef and vegetables are tender.

Lift the beef on to a carving board and transfer the vegetables to a warmed serving dish using a slotted spoon. Mix the cornflour with a little water to make a paste and stir it into the remaining sauce. Cover again and cook for a few minutes or until thickened.

Thickly slice the beef and divide between plates along with the vegetables and gravy. Scatter with the parsley to serve.

Don't have a slow cooker?

Put all the ingredients up to the thyme into a non-stick casserole pan or dish, cover and cook for 1 hour in an oven preheated to 160°C/fan 140°C/gas 3. Add the vegetables under the beef and cook for a further 1-1½ hours or until tender. Add the cornflour paste.

one for all | **go slow**

chinese black bean and pepper beef

serves 4

Free

ready in 8 hours 15 minutes

600g lean casserole/braising steak, visible fat removed, cut into strips

1 medium onion, halved and sliced

5cm piece fresh root ginger, peeled and shredded

4 garlic cloves, crushed

120ml boiling beef stock

4 tbsp dark soy sauce

1 tsp Chinese five-spice powder

½ tsp ground ginger

½ tsp garlic granules

½ level tsp sweetener granules

3 peppers (any colours), deseeded and sliced

400g can or carton black beans, drained and rinsed

225g can bamboo shoots, drained

225g can sliced water chestnuts, drained

chopped fresh chives, to serve

Everyone will love the mouth-watering aroma of a fantastic Free fakeaway bubbling away in your slow cooker… and they'll enjoy tucking in even more!

Put the steak, onion, ginger and garlic in the slow cooker pot and mix well.

Mix the stock with the soy sauce, spices, sweetener and ½ tsp black pepper and pour over the steak. Cover and cook on low for 8-10 hours.

About 1 hour before the end of the cooking time, stir in the remaining ingredients, cover again and cook until the steak is meltingly tender. Scatter with chives to serve. This is delicious with rice or noodles – or plain cauliflower rice if you want to keep it suitable for Extra Easy *SP*.

Don't have a slow cooker?

Put all the ingredients up to the sweetener in a non-stick casserole pan or dish, then cover and cook for 1½ hours in an oven preheated to 160°C/fan 140°C/gas 3. Stir in the remaining ingredients, cover and return to the oven for a further 1 hour or until tender.

one for all | **go slow**

lamb kleftiko

Our Food Optimising version of the classic Greek lamb dish is packed with authentic flavours.
If you want to make it completely Free, just leave out the feta.

Put the potatoes, red peppers, tomatoes, garlic, oregano, lemon juice, bay leaves, 1 tsp salt and some pepper in a mixing bowl and toss well.

Pick the potatoes out of the mixture and spread them out in the slow cooker pot. Season the lamb steaks and put them on top, then cover with the rest of the vegetable mixture. Pour over 150ml boiling water, cover and cook on low for 8-9 hours or until the lamb and potatoes are tender.

Scatter over the feta and parsley to serve.

Don't have a slow cooker?

Arrange all the ingredients except the feta and parsley in a large non-stick roasting tin, cover with foil and seal around the edges. Bake for 3 hours in an oven preheated to 190°C/fan 170°C/gas 5.

serves 4

1½ Syns per serving

❋ (without the cheese)

ready in 8 hours 15 minutes

1kg waxy potatoes such as Desiree, scrubbed and quartered lengthways

2 large red peppers, deseeded and cut into bite-size chunks

2 large tomatoes, thickly sliced

1 garlic bulb, cloves separated, peeled and halved

2 tsp dried oregano

4 tbsp lemon juice

4 bay leaves

600g lean lamb leg steaks, visible fat removed, halved

75g reduced-fat feta cheese, crumbled, to serve

chopped fresh parsley, to serve

risi e bisi

serves 4

Free

ready in 3 hours 15 minutes

---

1 medium onion, finely chopped

6 back bacon rashers, visible fat removed, chopped

3 garlic cloves, crushed

¼ tsp fennel seeds, lightly crushed

1.5 litres boiling vegetable stock

350g dried risotto rice, such as arborio

200g asparagus tips

8 spring onions, sliced

225g fresh or frozen peas

Turn your peas into VIPs with this comforting rice dish that's much-loved in Italy.

Put the onion, bacon, garlic, fennel seeds and 100ml stock in the slow cooker pot. Cover and cook on low for 2 hours.

Stir in the rice, asparagus, spring onions and the rest of the stock, cover again and cook for a further 1 hour, adding the peas for the final 20 minutes.

Serve with salad. (Sprinkle with freshly grated Parmesan cheese for a luxurious finish – 1 level tbsp is 1 Syn.)

Don't have a slow cooker?

Spray a large non-stick saucepan or casserole pan with low-calorie cooking spray and place over a low heat. Add the onion, bacon, garlic, fennel seeds and 100ml stock, cover and cook for 10 minutes. Uncover, add the rice, asparagus, spring onions and remaining stock and cook for 20-25 minutes or until tender, stirring now and then. Stir in the peas and simmer for 2-3 minutes.

mexican pork pozole

serves 4

Free

❄

ready in 8 hours 15 minutes

2 tsp ground cumin

1 tsp smoked paprika

½ tsp garlic granules

1kg lean pork loin joint, visible fat removed

1 large onion, chopped

½ tsp dried chilli flakes

½ level tsp chipotle chilli paste (or another chilli paste)

3 tbsp tomato purée

500ml boiling chicken stock

1 tsp dried oregano

340g can sweetcorn kernels in water, drained

400g can lentils, drained and rinsed

Our Free version of this tasty stew features oh-so-tender pork pulled apart and stirred into the sensational spicy sauce.

Mix the cumin, paprika, garlic granules and ½ tsp each salt and pepper in a shallow dish. Add the pork joint and turn to coat well. Put the onion and chilli flakes in the slow cooker pot and place the pork joint on top.

Mix the chilli paste, tomato purée, stock and oregano with any spices left in the pork dish. Pour the mixture over the pork, cover and cook on low for 8-10 hours.

After the pork has been cooking for 7-8 hours, stir in the sweetcorn and lentils. Cover again and cook for the rest of the cooking time or until the pork is very tender and starting to fall apart.

Lift the pork on to a board, pull it into strips using 2 forks and stir it back into the stew. Serve hot in bowls with salad.

Don't have a slow cooker?

Put all the ingredients except the sweetcorn and lentils in a non-stick casserole pan, cover and cook for 2-2½ hours in an oven preheated to 160°C/fan 140°C/gas 3. Add the sweetcorn and lentils, cover and return to the oven for a further 30 minutes.

split pea and ham soup

serves 4

Free

❄ (not the ham hock) *SP*

ready in 5 hours 15 minutes

500g dried yellow split peas

1 large onion, finely chopped

3 carrots, peeled and chopped

1 large leek, sliced

3 celery sticks, chopped

5 garlic cloves, crushed

2 bay leaves

1 tsp dried sage

1 tsp chopped fresh thyme leaves

1.5 litres boiling vegetable or chicken stock

200g shredded cooked lean ham hock (5% fat or less, available from the chiller cabinet in most supermarkets)

chopped fresh parsley, to serve

This traditional British soup is so satisfying – we've given it a twist by using shredded ham hock from the chiller counter for even more flavour.

Put the split peas, onion, carrots, leek, celery, garlic, bay leaves, sage, thyme, ½ tsp salt and some pepper in the slow cooker pot and stir to combine. Pour over the stock, cover and cook on high for 5-6 hours.

Remove and discard the bay leaves. Ladle half of the soup into a food processor or liquidiser, blend until smooth and stir back into the slow cooker pot. Check the seasoning, ladle into bowls and scatter over the ham hock and parsley to serve.

Don't have a slow cooker?

Put all the ingredients except the ham and parsley in a large saucepan or casserole pan, cover and simmer over a low heat for 1½ hours or until the split peas are tender.

chicken and mushroom fricassee

serves 4

½ **Syn** per serving

ready in 2 hours 45 minutes

2 large leeks, thickly sliced

3 large carrots, peeled and sliced

400g white or button mushrooms, halved or quartered

2 garlic cloves, crushed

1 tsp paprika

1 tbsp fresh thyme leaves, plus extra to serve

4 skinless and boneless chicken breasts, cut into small chunks

3 bay leaves

250ml boiling chicken stock

2 level tbsp cornflour

4 tbsp plain quark

Chicken and mushrooms were made for each other and this French-style favourite will go down a treat with the whole family.

Put the leeks, carrots, mushrooms and garlic in the slow cooker pot. Mix the paprika, thyme, ½ tsp salt and some pepper in a shallow dish then add the chicken and toss to coat well. Lay the chicken chunks on top of the vegetables, add the bay leaves and pour over the stock. Cover and cook on high for 2-2½ hours or until the chicken is almost tender.

Mix the cornflour with a little water to make a paste and stir it into the fricassee. Cover again and cook for 30 minutes or until thickened.

Stir the quark into the fricassee and scatter over the extra thyme. It's great served with swede mash.

Don't have a slow cooker?

Put all the ingredients up to the stock in a non-stick casserole pan, cover and cook for 1 hour in an oven preheated to 160°C/fan 140°C/gas 3. Stir in the cornflour paste, return to the oven and cook for a further 30 minutes or until the chicken is cooked.

asian barbecue chicken

serves 4

1 Syn per serving

ready in 2 hours 45 minutes

¼ tsp onion granules

¼ tsp garlic granules

½ tsp chilli powder

½ tsp paprika

2 tsp barbecue seasoning

8 large skinless chicken thighs, visible fat removed

3 garlic cloves, crushed

3cm piece fresh root ginger, peeled and grated

1 mild green chilli, deseeded and finely chopped

3 tbsp dark soy sauce

1 level tbsp sweetener granules

3 tbsp lemon juice

250g passata

1 level tsp chilli paste

1 level tbsp cornflour

2 spring onions, halved and shredded, to serve

1 level tsp sesame seeds, lightly toasted, to serve

Slow cooking concentrates the amazing flavours of this deeply savoury sauce – chicken has never tasted so good!

Mix the onion granules, garlic granules, chilli powder, paprika, barbecue seasoning, ½ tsp salt and ½ tsp freshly ground black pepper in a shallow dish. Add the chicken thighs, turn to coat well and put them in the slow cooker pot.

Mix the garlic, ginger, green chilli, soy sauce, sweetener, lemon juice, passata and chilli paste together and pour all over the chicken. Cover and cook on high for 2-2½ hours or until the chicken is almost tender.

Mix the cornflour with a little water to make a paste. Stir the cornflour paste into the sauce, cover again and cook on high for another 30 minutes or until the chicken is tender.

Sprinkle the chicken with the spring onions and sesame seeds to serve. This is fantastic with rice and Speed vegetables.

Don't have a slow cooker?

Put all the ingredients except the cornflour in a non-stick casserole pan, cover and cook for 1 hour in an oven preheated to 160°C/fan 140°C/ gas 3. Add the cornflour paste, cover and return to the oven for 15 minutes or until the chicken is cooked.

white chilli

If you like chilli con carne, you'll love this inventive recipe featuring generous chunks of chicken and filling cannellini beans.

Put the onion, green pepper, leek, celery, green chillies and garlic in the slow cooker pot.

Put the chilli powder, cumin, oregano, thyme, ½ tsp salt and some black pepper in a shallow dish and mix together, then add the chicken chunks and turn to coat well. Scatter the chicken chunks over the vegetables, pour over the stock and cook on high for 2-2½ hours or until the chicken is almost tender.

Mix the cornflour with a little water to make a paste and stir it into the chicken along with the beans. Check the seasoning, cover again and cook for a further 30 minutes.

Stir in the quark, scatter over the spring onions and add a splash of Tabasco sauce if you like a bit of heat. Serve hot.

Don't have a slow cooker?

Put all the ingredients up to the stock in a non-stick casserole pan, cover and cook for 1 hour in an oven preheated to 160°C/fan 140°C/gas 3. Add the cornflour paste and beans, cover and return to the oven for a further 30 minutes or until the chicken is cooked.

serves 4

½ **Syn** per serving

ready in 2 hours 45 minutes

---

1 large onion, chopped

1 large green pepper, deseeded and diced

1 large leek, sliced

4 celery sticks, sliced

2 mild green chillies, deseeded and chopped

3 garlic cloves, crushed

1 tbsp chilli powder (heat to your taste)

1½ tbsp ground cumin

1 tsp dried oregano

1 tbsp fresh thyme leaves

4 large skinless and boneless chicken breasts, cut into bite-size chunks

300ml boiling chicken stock

2 level tbsp cornflour

400g can cannellini beans, drained and rinsed

3 tbsp plain quark

sliced spring onions, to serve

splash of Tabasco sauce, to serve (optional)

jamaican seafood curry

Our slow-cooked supper brings together some of the Caribbean island's best-loved ingredients – it's sweet, spicy and sensational!

serves 4

2 Syns per serving

ready in 4 hours 10 minutes

Put the onion, garlic, ginger, chilli, spices, sweetener, chopped tomatoes, coconut milk and a little seasoning into the slow cooker pot. Stir well, cover and cook on high for 1 hour.

Add the okra, cover again and cook for another 2 hours.

Stir in the spinach, cherry tomatoes and prawns. Season the fish chunks lightly and lay them on top of the curry. Cover again and cook for a further 1 hour.

Stir in the lime juice and scatter over the extra spinach leaves. This is great served with rice.

Don't have a slow cooker?

Put all the ingredients up to the coconut milk in a large saucepan or casserole pan, season, cover and simmer over a low heat for 30 minutes. Add the okra, cover and simmer for 30 minutes. Stir in the spinach, cherry tomatoes and prawns then lay the fish on top. Cover and simmer for 5 minutes or until the prawns and fish are cooked through.

1 large onion, finely chopped

2 garlic cloves, crushed

5cm piece fresh root ginger, peeled and grated

1 medium-hot green chilli, deseeded and finely chopped

1 tbsp curry powder

½ tsp each ground cinnamon, dried chilli flakes and turmeric

¼ tsp ground cloves or allspice

2 tsp nigella seeds

1 level tsp sweetener granules

200g chopped tomatoes

200ml reduced-fat coconut milk

175g okra, each sliced into 3-4 pieces on the diagonal

100g baby leaf spinach, plus a few leaves to serve

200g cherry tomatoes, halved

200g raw peeled prawns

400g skinless and boneless firm white fish fillets, cut into large chunks

1 tbsp lime juice

five-a-day tagine with chermoula

This North African-style vegetable feast is made unforgettable thanks to the chermoula, a vibrant blend of spices and fresh herbs added during and after cooking.

Put the chickpeas, onions, celeriac, squash, swede, courgettes and cinnamon stick in the slow cooker pot.

Put all the chermoula ingredients into a small food processor, add ½ tsp salt and blend to a paste.

Mix the chopped tomatoes with the stock, ginger, lemon zest and half the chermoula paste (non-vegans can add 2 level tsp clear honey for extra flavour – adds ½ Syn per serving). Pour the tomato mixture over the vegetables, cover and cook on high for 4 hours or until the vegetables are tender.

About 10 minutes before the tagine is ready, put the couscous in a wide heatproof bowl, just cover with boiling water and cover with cling film. Leave for 10 minutes then fluff up the grains with a fork.

Discard the cinnamon stick from the tagine, stir in the olives, lemon juice and remaining chermoula and check the seasoning. Serve hot with the couscous.

Don't have a slow cooker?

Put all the ingredients up to the lemon into a non-stick casserole pan (including half the chermoula), cover and cook for 2 hours in an oven preheated to 160°C/fan 140°C/gas 3.

serves 4

½ **Syn** per serving

❄ (without the couscous)

 vegan

ready in 4 hours 20 minutes

400g can chickpeas, drained and rinsed

2 medium red onions, halved and sliced

1 medium celeriac, peeled and cut into small chunks

½ medium butternut squash, peeled, deseeded and cut into small chunks

1 large swede, peeled and cut into small chunks

2 courgettes, cut into small chunks

1 small cinnamon stick

400g can chopped tomatoes

350ml boiling vegetable stock

1 tsp ground ginger

3 pared strips unwaxed lemon zest, plus 2 tbsp lemon juice

350g dried couscous

12 pitted black olives in brine, drained

for the chermoula

½ small pack fresh mint

½ small pack fresh coriander

3 garlic cloves

2 tsp each ground cumin, ground coriander and paprika

1 red chilli, deseeded and chopped

pinch of saffron or ¼ tsp turmeric

spinach and ricotta lasagne

serves 6

2 Syns per serving

Ⓥ (if the cheese is vegetarian)

ready in 4 hours 20 minutes

---

2 x 350g pots Slimming World Creamy Tomato Sauce, thawed (or use 700g passata)

400g can chopped tomatoes

3 roasted red peppers in brine from a jar, drained and chopped

small pack fresh basil, shredded

¼ tsp dried chilli flakes (optional)

300g low-fat natural cottage cheese

100g ricotta cheese

4 level tbsp freshly grated Parmesan cheese or vegetarian alternative

9 dried lasagne pasta sheets, each snapped across into 4 pieces

2 medium courgettes, thinly sliced lengthways

100g baby leaf spinach, coarsely shredded

1 level tbsp cornflour

500g fat-free natural Greek yogurt

2 medium eggs, beaten

½ tsp freshly grated nutmeg

You'll be amazed how well a lasagne can work in your slow cooker, and the mix of ricotta and Parmesan is a real treat.

In a large bowl, mix the creamy tomato sauce or passata with the chopped tomatoes, peppers, basil, chilli, if using, and seasoning to taste.

In a smaller bowl, mix the cottage cheese with the ricotta, half the Parmesan and a little seasoning.

Spread about one-third of the tomato sauce mixture over the base of the slow cooker pot and cover with one-third of the lasagne sheets. Spread over half of the cottage cheese mixture, then half of the sliced courgettes and half of the chopped spinach. Repeat the layers once more then cover with the remaining lasagne sheets and tomato sauce. Cover and cook on low for 3 hours.

Mix the cornflour and a little yogurt in a bowl to make a paste then mix in the rest of the yogurt, the eggs, nutmeg, remaining Parmesan and a little seasoning to taste. Pour over the lasagne, cover again and cook for 1 hour.

If you want to brown the top of your lasagne, preheat your grill to high just before the end of the cooking time. Carefully lift out the slow cooker pot and put it under the grill for 5 minutes or until browned to your liking. Serve hot with salad.

Don't have a slow cooker?

Build up the layers as above but in a shallow ovenproof dish. Top with the yogurt mixture and bake for 45 minutes or until cooked through in an oven preheated to 200°C/fan 180°C/gas 6.

spicy veg and lentil curry

serves 4

Free

Ⓥ vegan

ready in 4 hours 20 minutes

---

2 carrots, peeled and cut into small chunks

1 large sweet potato, peeled and cut into small chunks

150g dried red lentils

1 large onion, chopped

400ml boiling vegetable stock

200g can chopped tomatoes

2 garlic cloves, crushed

1 medium-hot red chilli, deseeded and finely chopped

5cm piece fresh root ginger, peeled and grated

1 tbsp mild or medium curry powder

1 tsp paprika

1 tsp turmeric

1 tbsp ground cumin

12 curry leaves (optional)

1 large courgette, thickly sliced

1 small cauliflower, broken into small florets

100g green beans, each cut into 2-3 pieces

100g frozen peas

chopped fresh coriander, to serve

It's the warming spices that make this Free veggie curry so memorable and more-ish!

Layer the carrots and sweet potato in the slow cooker pot with the lentils, onion and a little seasoning.

Mix the stock with the tomatoes, garlic, chilli, ginger, all the spices and the curry leaves, if using. Pour the mixture over the carrots and sweet potato, cover and cook on high for 2 hours.

Stir in the courgette, cauliflower and green beans, cover again and cook for another 2 hours or until all the vegetables are tender, adding the peas for the final 20 minutes.

Check the seasoning and scatter over the coriander to serve.

Don't have a slow cooker?

Layer the carrots, sweet potato and lentils in a non-stick casserole pan and pour over the stock mixture. Cover and cook for 1 hour in an oven preheated to 160°C/fan 140°C/gas 3. Stir in the courgette, cauliflower and green beans, cover again and return to the oven for 1 hour or until tender, adding the peas for the last 20 minutes.

cook's tips

Our handy hints will help you keep your weight loss perfectly on track.

eggs

Pregnant women, the elderly, babies and toddlers are advised to choose eggs showing the British Lion stamp if eating raw or partially cooked eggs. We'll make a note in any recipes using them.

fat-free natural fromage frais, yogurt and plain quark

These are wonderful ingredients when you're Food Optimising as they give the creamy texture and taste normally achieved with cream. They make great savoury or sweet ingredients. Unless the recipe says otherwise, add them off the heat once all the other ingredients have been cooked and simply heat through.

fresh, canned and frozen

Frozen ingredients and canned veg and beans are great alternatives to fresh foods and are so handy to keep in the cupboard or freezer. They'll keep for much longer, can be quicker to cook and are just as good for you. So feel free to switch between all three – bear in mind cooking times may change slightly.

fruit

While most fresh whole fruit is Free, juiced, canned, puréed or cooked fruit counts as Syns because it isn't as filling and becomes easier to over-consume. Where fruit is puréed or cooked, we count it as Syns.

low-calorie cooking spray

Where you do need to use fat then choose a low-calorie cooking spray which contains 1 calorie or less per spray, as these are Free – others would need to be counted as Syns. Ideal for fried eggs, roast potatoes and chips!

meat and poultry

Trim off any visible fat before cooking to make lean meat or poultry Free, and remember to remove the skin before or after cooking poultry. If you cook poultry with the skin on, we'd advise cooking it separately from the other ingredients so that the fat can't run into them (eg. don't roast potatoes in the same tin).

meat and poultry – mince

Lean minced meat (5% fat or less) is a Free Food. Beef, pork and turkey mince are available in most major supermarkets at 5% fat or less – check the nutrition information to be sure. If possible, drain off any fat that comes from the mince while you're cooking it. No chicken and lamb mince is widely available with 5% fat or less so these would have a Syn value… unless you fancy mincing it yourself or you know a friendly butcher.

mustard powder

Made-up mustard in jars has Syns because it contains Synned ingredients while mustard powder is Free, making it a great choice for dressings and sauces.

non-stick pans

To cut down on fat in recipes, we recommend using non-stick cookware/bakeware wherever possible.

seasoning

Where salt and pepper are used, we usually suggest seasoning to taste (you might not need any at all). Official advice is that adults should eat no more than 6g of salt a day – and small amounts can quickly add up. Go for reduced-salt products to reduce your intake.

slow cooking

There's nothing like a slow cooker for making easy Food Optimising meals with the maximum flavour and the minimum fuss!

Buying: Slow cookers come in various sizes so choose one that fits your needs best, whether you're cooking for one or feeding a large family. Whatever you're cooking, your food should fill at least half the pot. All the recipes in this book have been tested in a standard-size slow cooker with a capacity of 3.5 litres.

Cooking: As a rule, the high setting will take just over half the cooking time of the low setting. Try to resist the temptation to lift the lid during cooking. As your food cooks, steam will condense on the lid and trickle back into the pot – this helps produce a seal, which is broken each time you lift the lid.

Cleaning: Once you have finished cooking, always turn off the slow cooker before lifting out the pot. To prolong the life of your slow cooker, it's best not to wash the pot or lid straight away. Eat your meal and allow it to cool slightly before washing in hot, soapy water.

stock

Fresh stock, stock cubes, stock pots, bouillon powder, ready-to-use liquid stock and liquid stock concentrate are all Free but be aware that gravy granules or powder and stock granules are not. Stock should normally be boiling when you add it to the pan, as cold stock will slow down cooking times.

syn measurements

Syns for some ingredients are based on level teaspoons or tablespoons. Without measuring carefully, it's easy to far exceed your intended Syn intake without realising – so scrape a knife along the top of the spoon, knocking the excess back into the container. For best results, invest in a set of measuring spoons.

symbol sense

serves…

This gives you an idea of how many people the recipe can serve. However, feel free to split the recipe between more or fewer people instead, depending on how hungry you are – especially when it's Free!

freezer-friendly ❄

Recipes showing this symbol can be safely frozen for up to 1 month. Keep in mind official advice on freezing safely:

- Label food for the freezer with details of what the meal is and when you cooked it.

- Make sure food has cooled before you put it in the freezer.

- Defrost frozen meals completely and reheat thoroughly before eating.

Batch cooking: Wherever you see the freezer-friendly symbol ❄, you can save time and effort by cooking double or triple amounts and freezing the rest to enjoy at a later date. You'll usually save money too because it's often cheaper to buy ingredients in bulk.

suitable for vegetarians Ⓥ / vegans vegan

Recipes with these symbols are suitable for vegetarians and vegans but we'd always recommend checking the packaging to be sure. For example, some cheeses come in vegetarian and non-vegetarian forms. And while most bread and dried pasta is suitable for vegans, it's always a good idea to check.

Extra Easy SP

For super-charged weight loss, go for dishes marked Extra Easy SP. See your Food Optimising book or ask your Consultant for more details.

ready in…

This gives a guide to how long the recipe will take to prepare and cook.

index